Hate Vanquished, Lives Remembered

Hate Vanquished, Lives Remembered

A Survivor's Story

CHARLOTTE ARPADI BAUM

LIBRARY *of the* HOLOCAUST

Washington, D.C.

Printed in the United States of America
ISBN: 978-1-88232615-0 (print)
Library of Congress Control Number: 2021939144

Library of the Holocaust Foundation
PO Box 1651
Silver Spring, Maryland 20915
(800) 651-9350
www.LibraryoftheHolocaust.org

Contents

The Beginning

My mother, Anna Ehrman, came to Berlin, Germany in 1921 to marry my father, Stephan Arpadi. Some friends of my father met my mother while visiting in Lithuania and were so impressed with her that they suggested that she might make a suitable wife for him. My father had entertained the thought of getting married, but had not yet met a girl who suited him, so he decided to follow their advice. He travelled to get acquainted with her and met her at her friend's home. My mother never could make up her mind quickly, and this time, when my father asked if she would marry him, was no exception. Her friend encouraged her to make her decision soon and teased her, saying that if my mother would not marry him, she had a string of girls who were anxious to do so. Well, that did it! The following day, when entering the dining room, she kept one of her hands conspicuously under her apron. After some prodding to show her hand, she bashfully held up her hand which sported a beautiful engagement ring.

1

Anna was born in 1891, in Gargždai, a typical East European shtetl, in Lithuania. This little border town was also known by the name of Garsden or Gorzdy and was called Gorzd by the Jewish population. The region was generally called East Prussia, depending on which country had control of the area at the time. Because of the location she grew up speaking four languages, Lithuanian, German, Russian, and Yiddish; the latter was spoken at home. She taught school in all of these languages in Gargzdai's only school.

My grandfather, Isaak Ehrman, was born in Odessa, Ukraine. In Gorzd, he manufactured bricks and seemed to have had a fairly good income to support a family of nine in comfort. My grandmother, the former Sarah Luntz, was known for her charity and was held in high esteem by the townspeople. In fact, I became an indirect recipient of her generosity.

When I was married, I received a most generous wedding gift from a friend of my mother, Dora Smaller. Later, at the birth of each of my sons I received boxes which contained half a dozen each of pants, shirts and sweaters. Dora told me that she and nine siblings came from a very poor home and that there was never enough food in the house. My grandmother often provided food for them, but she did it in such a way as not to shame them. She often asked Dora to come to the house to assist her with a few chores and then sent her home with bags of food for the family. After Dora came to the USA, she married and became quite affluent. She told me that inasmuch as my mother, at this time, did not need anything, she decided that I should be the recipient of her gratitude to my grandmother.

My mother had four brothers, George, Elias, Isaak and Benno. Elias loved sports and became a physical education teacher at the same school at which my mother taught. He was then known as, what we now would call, a "polar bear." Nothing would keep him from bathing in freezing or ice-covered waters, exhorting everyone to follow his lead. He later acquired a newspaper stand in Memel, now known as Klaipeda. He was a socialist and quite active during the Russian revolution during which he collected money from affluent people to support soup kitchens for the poor. After seeing the film "Dr. Zhivago" in the mid-1960s, my mother pointed to a particular scene and told me that Elias also had assisted with the hiding of guns used in the revolution.

Isaak, who had fiery red hair, dealt in flax and horses and was often away from home. Benno was the odd one in the family, today we would probably call him a drifter. The family, though, always cared and talked lovingly about him, saying that he used to be a bright, young boy until the day he fell from a roof he had climbed on. After this accident, his personality started to change as he became withdrawn. I do not remember him well because by the time we were old enough to travel to Gorzd, he no longer lived at home. I was assured, though, that he loved us and was too shy to meet us when we were visiting the grandparents. I was also told that he would come to the house and peek through the windows in order to catch a glimpse of us.

I never met my uncle George, as he already had left

Gorzd to live in New York. He married Esther and had two sons, Robert and Seneca, but died shortly after turning 50. Seneca and I have kept up our friendship and we have seen each other every so often at family celebrations or when visiting our respective towns. He lives in Tucson, Arizona.

I remember my aunt Hennie as fun loving and that she had spent lots of time with me when we came to visit. Aunt Gitta, the youngest of the girls, moved to Berlin after she got married. My mother, like many of the women in Gorzd, was basically a matchmaker at heart and was always on the lookout for husbands for her sisters. Once, when she bought flowers at the store across the street from our apartment in Berlin, she met the owner of the store and they started to talk to each other. My mother mentioned her unmarried sisters. By coincidence, the other lady had a bachelor brother looking for a bride. As he was a short man, Gitta, the smaller one of the two sisters, was chosen to date him and on our next visit to the grandparents, Paul Frankel accompanied us. They seemed to get along very well and one day, at the beach, when I noticed that they were kissing each other, I was told that they were engaged.

My mother was the first girl born after three boys and enjoyed the reputation of the girl most likely to succeed. The family doted on her and was proud of her accomplishments; I always had the impression that she was treated like a princess. She was the first girl in her town who would go to a higher institute of learning in another country, to Libau (Liepaja) in Latvia.

Stephan, my father was born in Berlin and owned a

Hungarian restaurant. His parents, Maria and Lajos, were originally from Szeged, Hungary, and had opened the restaurant in 1877. It was called Eszterhazy Keller, meaning Eszterhazy Cellar, for it was situated one short flight of stairs below street level at 114 Friedrich Strasse. Eszterhazy was a well-known Hungarian count. My father had one brother, Siegfried, and two sisters, Lisbeth and Gisela. Siegfried and Gisela, both lived in an apartment one floor above the restaurant, and helped my father run it. Lisbeth was married to a non-Jew by the name of Reich and also lived in Berlin. Our restaurant was open at least 18 hours a day and the family took turns supervising it; my father usually was the one to open it, Gisela could always be found in the kitchen in the early morning and later on, my mother would take over at the cash register.

Our restaurant's specialty was Hungarian Goulash. This dish was prepared after a recipe from a cookbook my grandparents Lajos and Maria Arpadi had published. There was a great variety of customers who frequented our place. In the early morning, taxi drivers or workers finishing their shifts would come in; later, at all hours, one could find guests who came frequently and would play cards at a table reserved for them. After the theaters closed, there again, our restaurant fulfilled a need.

There was a wine cellar and of course, a bar which served many kinds of drinks. Beer was always served from the tap. A small band, called Schrammel Band, consisting of a violin, accordion and piano, played in the evening. Many of the guests returned often and my fa-

5

ther, who was well liked, was asked to have a drink with them. He never tolerated more than one drink per night and, finally, he learned how to nurse one throughout the entire evening without being discovered. One section of the restaurant provided booths that sheltered the guests on both sides from the view of others and made dining more intimate.

I was born in 1922 and my brother Harry, in 1924. We enjoyed a happy childhood until 1933 when Hitler came to power. My upbringing conformed to the concept of a traditional, Jewish household, strictly kosher, for my mother followed all the dietary laws. My father, who did not have any preference in that regard, abided by all the rules and regulations that my mother and he agreed on concerning our religious education. In fact, my father's upbringing was such that he considered himself a German who happened to be born to Jewish parents. His knowledge of Judaism was almost nonexistent; his parents not believing it to be an integral part of his education.

A teacher, Michael Kern, came to the house to instruct us in the Hebrew language. My mother observed all the Jewish holidays and it was she who took us to the synagogue on the Oranienburger Strasse. This magnificent building, built in 1866 and designed like a mosque, was huge and elaborately decorated in blue and gold. Women and men were segregated, the women sat upstairs and the men downstairs. Sometimes, my father good naturedly dropped in a few minutes before the end of the services ended. I believe he humored my mother so she could point him out to the woman sitting next to her: "Oh, there is my husband!" She just wanted it to be known that he, too was observant. We also belonged to a small, very orthodox synagogue, located a couple of blocks from our apartment, which my mother would go to at other times. Occasionally, I would join her there, too.

We were the pride and joy of our parents and the only punishment I remember for misbehaving, was facing a corner of a room. For special occasions, until I was about six years old, Harry and I were dressed identically. Our clothes for festive occasions, sewn by a seamstress, were of silk or velvet, and for summer, cotton; the only difference was pants for Harry and skirts for me. Before we were of school age, a nanny took care of us and supervised us on our daily trips to various parks where she would sit with other nannies who socialized while we were doing the same with our peer group.

Whenever my father could spare some time, he took us for walks to the famous Tiergarten, a big park which started at one end of Under den Linden after passing through the Brandenburger Gate. Several outdoor cafes offered all kinds of snacks hungry children like us could not resist, especially if they had a father who always asked what we wanted. My favorite was hot chocolate covered with a lot of whipped cream.

When we asked him why he was bald, he told us that because he had to wear a helmet during the war, his hair eventually stopped growing. And we believed him. He also told us of the time, when courting our mother, that he went for a walk with Uncle Isaak. A man who was walking behind them seemed to follow them for some time and when questioned by my uncle as to his motives, asked my father several questions in Russian which my uncle translated: "Were you in the war? Were you a guard in a prisoner of war camp in Kassel? Did you guard Russian prisoners? Do you remember giving me cigarettes?" It turned out that this man was one of the prisoners the Germans had taken during World War I and whom my father had guarded. This little episode describes some of my father's attitudes toward life: he was generous and his motto was to live and let live. He was always cheerful, and he enjoyed life to the fullest. When we were on vacation, he would wake me with the first rays of the sun in the sky, practically singing that the sun was up, the birds were singing and that it was a beautiful morning. And this almost 20 years before he ever heard Oklahoma's "Oh what a beautiful morning...."

We lived a short distance from the restaurant; all we had to do to get there was to cross the street, walk about 300 feet and then turn around the corner. Until I was about six years old, we lived several flights up in the rear building. We could only reach our apartment by crossing the courtyard. We then moved to the front building to what was considered a choice apartment: three rooms on the first floor, with a bay window in the living room and a balcony which opened from my parent's bedroom. In warm weather, we spent many enjoyable hours on it. Depending on the season, boxes all around were planted with a variety of plants. In summer, my mother would plant a variety of flowering beans which she would train on strings so that complete privacy was achieved, hiding us from the view of our neighbors.

One flight up, on the other side of the building, lived another Jewish family, George and Flora Gross along with her mother, Mrs. Bachrach. George not only was a dentist but also sold dental supplies from his apartment, which was double size. The front, similar to ours, accommodated the business; the living quarters extended L-shaped toward the rear building. Being childless, the Grosses' viewed us as part of their family and I cannot remember a moment of my childhood without their presence; we considered them as our relatives and referred to them as our Uncle and Aunt. All three were patient with us as well as loved and spoiled us. George Gross was also our dentist. We spent much time in their apartment and my brother remembered how he was allowed to play with pieces of gold that was part of the dental supply. Flora's sister, Meta, was able to emigrate to England and from her we heard that George and Flora, having despaired of ever surviving the war, committed suicide by taking poison before they had to board a transport to an extermination camp.

Our location was most convenient for us, for there were trolley and bus stops just a few steps away. Across from the restaurant was the subway and the train station, Bahnhof Friedrich Strasse, which could be reached in less than 10 minutes. Most important for me, of course, was the movie theater across the street and an ice cream parlor next to it where one could watch how ice cream was made. Our big treat, on Sunday afternoons, was to watch a movie and then to buy some ice cream. A big indoor swimming pool was only a couple of blocks away. I went there fairly often and taught myself to swim and to jump off different heights of boards, trying to overcome my fear of doing so. There also was a candy store located next to the bus station, which was a real temptation when waiting for a bus. My great ambition in those early years was to own an ice cream parlor in summer and a candy store in winter.

I had a choice of two different routes to get to my school. One would lead me past our restaurant and was also the route I took most often. I made time to come in through the back entrance that led me directly to the kitchen which was humming with activities. We served breakfast and it

Charlotte with her aunt Gitta

was cooked to order. I understood that the coffee we served was very good and was appreciated by our regular guests. I was often allowed to set up the coffee service: a small, silver plated can, cup and saucer, creamer, sugar and a small teaspoon. I believe we must have served demi-tasse.

I always made enough time to read the newspaper, specifically one part of it that was important to me in those days: the daily installment of a current, romantic novel. I passionately loved reading books and as there were no public libraries, I was able to obtain books from a nearby lending library, a store located on Friedrich Strasse. There, for a nominal fee, I could take books out for a limited time. I was fascinated by reading of foreign countries and would read every book the library had on a specific country, and then select books on another one.

Uncle Siegfried had provided me at an early age with the opportunity to enjoy music. At the age of 10, he took me to see to opera "Hansel and Gretel" and shortly afterwards, "The Tales of Hoffman" by Offenbach. From then on, I became a lifelong devotee to operas. Whenever possible, I got up at dawn to be at the head of the line that formed in front of the Staats Opera in order to get tickets for the following week. Many Sunday mornings I would spend in the dark, huddled in blankets to ward off the cold and sipping a hot drink from a thermos bottle, waiting for the box office to open at 10 am; a three to four hour wait was the norm. Tickets for Saturday night performances were quickly sold out and my budget allowed me to buy standing room only, hence the necessity to be one of the first in line when tickets went on sale. One performance in particular which my friend Karla and I attended in March 1938 I have never forgotten. During intermission the "Annexation" of Austria was announced. The crowd cheered wildly!

When school closed in summer, we spent our vacation in different locations. My mother would rent a place for sometimes more than a month in Swinemuende or Kolberg, resort towns which were located on the Ost Sea (Baltic). These towns were not too far from Berlin, enabling my father to visit us for a few days. Our days were spent at the beach or on boardwalks and at dusk we would listen to outdoor music.

Another time, we went to what would be called now children's camp, except that the facilities were not as primitive, the life not quite so rustic and the supervision somewhat stricter than the ones in the States. I remember that we had to take short naps after lunch. The facility was located in Wyk on the island of Foehr in the North Sea. The dunes and white beaches were beautiful, and I was always fascinated by the changing of the tides. We would put our towels down near the edge of the sea and then go swimming. A few minutes later, when we looked for our towels, we would find them several feet away from the water, unnoticed, we had been going out slowly with the tide. One also could walk during low tide to other islands, but extreme care was needed to avoid miscalculating the incoming tide. There were stories about some unfortunate people who drowned before reaching their destination. I had always pictured that the water would just roll back during high tide but it never happened this way. First, the water started to percolate out of little holes in the sand, then it would slowly flood the whole area. How frightening this must have been to anyone who could not reach dry land in time.

Gorzd

For many of the summers we would go to Gorzd to visit my mother's family. It felt like everyone there was our family, for Harry and I were welcomed most warmly wherever we went. We made friends with other children and so did not suffer a lack of playmates. One of our playmates, whose house we sometimes were invited to, was Dr. Oxman's son David, who later went to Israel and married the daughter of Prime Minister Ben-Gurion.

Gorzd consisted of a market place, a few dirt side-streets, and a long main street of cobbled stone on which mostly merchants and traders lived. The street dipped to a neighborhood of the rickety homes of artisans, dairymen, peddlers, shoemakers, bakers, and butchers. Gorzd also boasted of a leather tannery and a blacksmith whom I had often watched putting new shoes on horses. The spacious market place was ringed with food, textile, and hardware stores, as well as a pharmacy and a tavern. Beyond the church, at the edge of the market place, one was already out of town. This road, which curved downhill, lead to the river Minya. Often, we would escape the heat to bathe there in the cool waters, shaded by groves of trees from the sun. This river was used to transport wood and, at times, one could see tree trunks floating to unknown destinations as far as eyes could reach. A short distance out of Gorzd was my grandfather's brick plant, which seems a bit grandiose considering it consisted of a pit with clay, a facility to form and dry bricks, and a kiln to fire them. The clay was mixed, to my great chagrin, by a horse which went around the pit in circles until the desired consistency was reached.

The two-story house in which my family lived could be entered by walking up a few steps to a small porch which led to the living room from which the two bedrooms and kitchen could be reached. The kitchen accommodated a big oven in which bread was baked every week. In big tubs the dough was prepared overnight and then baked the following day. Using wooden paddles several feet long, the bread was pushed into the oven and the delicious and tantalizing odor of freshly baked bread permeated the whole house. In the back of the kitchen, a big, unheated utility room provided space, not only for storing homemade jams and pickles, but also for making butter and cheese. Big bowls of milk were set up on benches. After several days, the milk turned sour and the cream was skimmed off; some of it was used as sour cream, and some was churned in a wooden butter churner to provide us with fresh butter. The left over liquid was buttermilk. This was boiled, poured through a triangular cheesecloth and then pressed between wooden paddles;

this then would turn out to be a delicious cheese similar to what is known now as farmers cheese. I was often allowed to help with these chores but looked forward to be sent to the bakery across the street for some of the still warm bagels.

The tantalizing aroma of freshly baked goods and being permitted to watch the process of baking bagels made this a favorite place to visit at other times as well. A door from the utility room led to the backyard. To the left there was a vegetable garden, situated right under the kitchen window. Straight ahead was the outhouse and further back, the stable for cows and horses. I can still hear the clanging tone the latch made when the door fell shut after it was opened. I have not forgotten an incident, which I always thought was very funny, concerning Harry when he was quite young. One day, when he emerged out of the outhouse, a rooster started chasing him. The picture he made was hilarious: his pants, which had the drop seat common for little boys, were not buttoned up but hung loose as he ran screaming through the yard with the rooster in pursuit. I am sure that Harry, at that time, did not think it funny.

Thursday was market day when peasants from surrounding towns came to sell their wares in the market. Vegetables, fruit, dairy, fish, and fowl were on display. To keep butter fresh, it was wrapped in large, green leaves. The chickens were still alive; the selection was made by turning it over, blowing the feathers at the tail end to reveal the amount of fat it had. On Fridays, the women would turn into demons, scrubbing the wooden floors and cooking traditional food for the Sabbath, which not only included Friday night dinner but also Saturday noon meal, which was kept hot in an oven, for no one was allowed to make a fire on Sabbath. And what a production it was; fish was chopped for gefilte fish, a very time consuming project which was part of the weekly ritual. An aura of frenzy hung over the village as everyone tried to get ready in time before sunset.

My mother sometimes told us about life in Gorzd. Much of it I have forgotten, but I still remember some. Many young men were mortally afraid to be inducted into the army, for as Jews, they did not fare well in the Russian army, being singled out for harsh treatment. They were very successful in reducing their weight to such a degree that they looked too emaciated and weak to be even considered for the draft. And how did they accomplish this? Their diet consisted mostly of lean beef.

Gorzd was a border town and my mother told us of the time during World War I, when Russian soldiers marched into the village and came to the house to occupy it. To the family they said: "Do not worry, no harm will come to you." They spread straw on the living room floor and went to sleep. After a couple of days they announced: "We are leaving now, but watch out, the Germans are coming!" They did and the previous scenario repeated itself. Again, the family was assured that no harm would befall them and now German soldiers slept in the living room. The family, as before, had to step over sleeping soldiers when going to the outhouse at night.

Sometimes we went to Memel (Klaipeda), an important

harbor about 10.5 miles from Gorzd. This harbor was not only used by major shipping lines in commerce but also by luxury liners docked there. We would either take a bus or go with Uncle Isaak in his horse drawn buggy, if he happened to go in that direction. There, we would visit with relatives and friends. The family would also rent a vacation home in Schwartzort or Sandkrug for several weeks. They were located on a peninsula with beaches at the edge of the Baltic Sea. To reach either one, a ferry from Memel would take us to a narrow strip of land on the other side of the harbor. To get to the beaches, we would walk from our cottage through a densely wooded area consisting of pine trees, until we came to the dunes, which we descended to get to the sea. The forest, with its wonderful pine scent, also provided us with a selection of most tasty mushrooms which I learned to recognize; regrettably they do not grow in America.

A few miles further west began a bay, an inlet of water, bordered on the ocean side by high dunes and on the land side by woods. Moonlight excursions on small boats were offered and one could observe majestic elks walking the crest of the dunes, a vision I have never forgotten. On some afternoons, one could participate in cultural events; I once won a trophy, a crystal vase, by correctly answering a music quiz naming the short excerpt played as Tchaikovsky's Fifth Symphony.

My thoughts often returned to Gorzd, for as I matured I would take different impressions of their way of life with me after every visit. Their steady belief in God -- in times of joy and sorrow, nothing would mar this personal identification. I can attest to this, having seen my mother's unshakable devotion to her God. There was a deep sense of community commitment; people shared each other's joys and troubles. Young people of the shtetl would take turns spending the night at the homes of sick people who had no one to care for them. If there was a need for food, all the Jews would make sure that the family would be adequately supplied with it. They supported the families of the ones who studied the Torah on a fulltime basis.

The townspeople had a deep feeling of trust in their rabbi and other wise and learned people who helped set the standards for proper behavior in the community. They were the arbitrators and mediators when people came to an impasse in a situation which called for objectivity and good judgement. Poverty and adversity was often treated with humor; could this perhaps have made it more bearable? Much of the humor in Yiddish is difficult to translate, often just an inflection of voice would change the entire meaning.

Always observed were an abiding respect and obedience to parents, and the obligation the children took upon themselves to make sure that they were taken care of in their old age. From my earliest childhood I remember the following story: An old man lived with his son, his daughter in-law and their little boy. As he became more feeble, his hands began to shake and sometimes at mealtimes he would drop the bowl he was eating from and it would break. He then was given a bowl made of wood. One day, the young father observed his son whittling a piece of wood and asked him what he is doing. The boy replied to this: "I am making a wooden bowl for you to eat from when you get to be old like grandfather."

Standing out in my mind is the impression I had of the people's deep compassion, tolerance and understanding of people's mental and physical handicaps. Only now do I recognize that a part of me was shaped through my heritage of Gorzd.

The Destruction of Gorzd

When the Nazis broke their treaty with the U.S.S.R., the German army opened its offensive against the Russians. One of the first places attacked was Gorzd, situated on the border. At that time, the population of Gorzd numbered 3000 residents, of whom 600-700 were Jews. Among them were Jews who had moved from the city of Memel in March 1939, when the whole of the Memel District was annexed by Germany. The Nazis attacked Gorzd on June 22, 1941 at 3 a.m. They encountered strong resistance by the Russians, but by 3 p.m., Gorzd was in German hands. They then rounded up all the Jews and brought them to the market place. From there, they herded them into the city park where they remained for the night. On the following day, they were all transported to an area outside Gorzd where they stayed until the next morning. Then, the women and children were taken to the village Anelishke and all adult Jewish males, numbering 200, were brought to a field.

On an order given by the German Command, policemen were brought from the cities of Memel and Tilsit. The police were told that the Jews had attacked the German army and were sentenced to death by firing squad. The brutal execution was fixed for June 24. The Germans demanded that all money and valuables they had in their possession be handed over. After they were ordered to remove their coats, the Nazis forced a few to collect the corpses of Russian soldiers, others were ordered to dig defense trenches or widen existing ones.

The Nazis prepared this execution to the last detail. They took their victims to a long ditch that would be their grave, which they had to dig themselves, and lined them up in front of it. The victims, in groups of 10, were ordered to turn and face the firing squad, which numbered about 20 Germans, two for each victim. Former residents of Memel recognized some of the policemen, one saw a former neighbor and friend standing opposite him with rifle pointed towards him. The German policemen brutally prodded each group closer to the ditch of death and forced them to roll the corpses of those already murdered into it. Were my uncles Elias and Isaak murdered on that day?

The women and children, who were taken to Anelishke, were subjected for several months to hard labor. In September 1941, they were driven to the Ashmanian woods, near the road leading from Gorzd to Kul. There, the Germans seized the children from their mothers and killed them on the spot. The mothers and the rest of the women were massacred by them two days later. Rachel Yami of Gorzd, who was with the women in Anelishke, was the only one who succeeded in escaping. Were Uncle Isaak's wife Goldie and their two young sons, who were not yet five years old, among the victims on that day?

Berlin 1933 - 1939

As the years passed, more laws were passed in regards to education of Jewish children who were allowed to go only to Jewish schools. I was taken out of the Queen Louise Lyceum and transferred to an exclusively Jewish school, the Grosse Hamburger School. In front of the school stood the bust of the philosopher Moses Mendelsohn. His grave was located in back of the school and was accessible through a gate of the courtyard where we spent our recesses.

Still more laws were passed restricting our activities. When Jewish artists were excluded from the general cultural life, the "Juedischer Kulturbund" (Jewish Cultural Association) was established in 1935. Many famous Jewish artists who were ousted from the general theater performed now in productions staged entirely by Jews and for Jews. I held season tickets and attended a variety of theater and music performances. I do remember the summer of 1936, when the Olympic Games were held in Berlin. My brother and I would have dearly loved to view but were, as Jews, forbidden to do so. We were both interested in sports, belonged to a sports organization, and regularly attended activities in a stadium in Grunewald used only by Jews. In fact, Harry received honors in short distance running. We once set out to go ice skating and after arriving at the rink, my brother needed to fix a strap. When he looked up, he noticed the sign that forbade Jews to skate and we left immediately. Restaurants and parks posted signs that said "Jews and Dogs not permitted here."

Every so often we would hear that the Nazis arrested some men and sent them to a concentration camp in Oranienburg, outside Berlin. If anyone did return, he would never tell of his experience, having signed a document to that effect, or risked being arrested again. We never knew the full story. Some never returned and their families, upon payment, might receive their ashes.

In the summer of 1938 a meeting to discuss the plight of the Jews was held in Evian, Switzerland. It was attended by close to 30 nations, including the United States, and although all expressed their sympathy with the victims of the German persecution, voiced their inability to increase immigration quotas to their countries. The world had abandoned us!

We were allowed to keep our passports but it was stamped with a "J". We also received new middle names; women had to add "Sarah" and the men "Israel" after their first name.

And so we come to the Kristallnacht, "The Night of Broken Glass," on November 9, 1938. An apt name, as the windows of Jewish stores throughout Germany and Austria were smashed and the streets were littered with broken glass. Jewish homes were broken in; windows, dishes, and furniture smashed. No accurate account of the damage to Jewish property exists, but it has been estimated conservatively that 30,000 Jews were arrested and sent to concentration camps; 300 Jews were killed; close to 8000 Jewish shops and businesses destroyed; 191 synagogues burned and another 110 completely demolished. This night marked the beginning of what would later be called the "Final Solution"; the Holocaust had really begun.

The official explanation was that the devastation of the Kristallnacht was in direct response to the assassination of Ernst von Rath, a German attaché in Paris, by Herschel Grynszpan, a 17-year old Polish-Jewish refugee. Grynszpan's family was deported to Poland under the most terrible conditions and were suffering greatly. He was frustrated that all his attempts to help them failed and resorted to violence to call the world's attention to his plight and was happening to the Jews in Germany. The ensuing rampage was not spontaneous, it was an organized pogrom known to the leaders of the Nazi Party. In fact, Josef Goebbels was not only responsible of ordering and encouraging this "action," but also of specifically instructing to how this was to be carried out.

My father was on friendly terms with many people in our area, among them the precinct police, as our restaurant was well known. At dawn on that morning my father received a call from the police chief, warning him not to open the restaurant, which my father was in the habit of doing every day at 6 a.m. The police chief warned him that his life might be endangered. My father, not realizing the extent of the seriousness of his situation, did not listen and proceeded to open the door, not knowing that a mob was waiting outside ready to attack him and to destroy our restaurant. He managed to slam the door shut, escaped through the back entrance and came home. Fortunately we lived around the corner, a short walk from the business. The brown shirted SA men, equipped with guns, tore through the streets looking for Jewish men and my father was lucky that he was not killed. We did not dare to stay in our apartment for fear that the SA men might still be looking for him. Elderly neighbors offered to hide my father and my brother in their apartment. These kind, courageous Germans, whose name was Vanderbank, lived a few floors above us. One of our employees, a lovely lady, agreed to hide my mother and me and we spent several days in an attic space. We felt safe with her; her husband was a member of the Nazi party. His uniform hung in the closet - he was a Nazi in name only.

To add injustice to injury, all Jews were held responsible for the damage, cleaning up the mess which had occurred during Krystallnacht and providing financial restitution to the government for the damage done. Not only were they fined 1 billion marks – about $400 million -- but also had to hand over jewelry, silver, furs and family valuables. Any Jew who owned a business or home had to sell it cheaply or when this failed the business would be "Aryanized" - taken over by non-Jewish Germans. All this was required before anyone was allowed to emigrate. There was no buyer for our restaurant, but I remember that my father sold some of the furniture. The restaurant closed and never reopened.

We had made plans to emigrate to the United States and were on the waiting list because the quotas for this year were already filled. My parents had no more illusions and knowing that we could not wait another one or two years and that time was running out, tried frantically to find a country that would accept us. They applied for and received a visa to Shanghai, China. Earlier that year my mother's sister, Gittel, her husband Paul Frankel, and three year old son, Erwin, were able to secure passage to La Paz, Bolivia. Paul was in danger of immediate arrest and was lucky to have been able to emigrate on such short notice.

After securing passage, we had sold most of our household goods, when suddenly we received a visa to Riga, Latvia, where my mother's cousin, Rebecca Gottlieb resided. We were elated by this sudden turn of events for we had been extremely unhappy at the thought of having to live in Shanghai. Rebecca told us how the issue of the Latvian visa came about. Dubin, a Jew and former Parliament official, had recently celebrated his birthday, and was visited by Latvian President Ullmanis, a good friend of his. Ullmanis told him that he did not bring him a present but asked him what he wanted for his birthday. Dubin mentioned a list with 100 names of German Jews with relatives in Latvia who wanted to immigrate. Ullmanis honored this request and we were on this list.

The telegram notifying us that permission to come to Riga was granted arrived on the day my father and brother had brought 17 pieces of luggage to the Friedrich Strasse Bahnhof Station. We were to leave for Genoa, Italy, to board the "Conte Biancomano" destined to sail for Shanghai. They went back to the station and were able to retrieve the luggage immediately. I remember our last night in Berlin, when we fearfully slept in our empty apartment, burning some leftover chairs to keep us warm. We left Berlin on January 29, 1939, afraid to remain another day. January 30 was celebrated as the anniversary of day Hitler rose to power and one never knew what "surprises" were planned for the Jews.

R

Riga 1939 - 1941

In Riga, I was able to secure jobs, mostly supervising children with their studies, foreign languages, piano, and organizing games when going to the playground. My brother also found some work and our combined income, with some assistance from the Jewish community, helped us survive. Toward the end of 1939, Russian troops marched into the Baltic states and annexed Estonia, Latvia, and Lithuania.

Charlotte and her mother, Riga 1939

Arpadi family, Riga 1939

I started to date Harry's boss, Eugene Borkum. My parents feared that I was getting serious about him and decided that I was not to go out with him again. It was the first time I dated and I had a carefree, good time, and if I had not thought of our relationship as serious until now, the restrictions and pressures brought upon me forced me to reconsider the situation. By the time our visas for the United States were issued, I was convinced that I was in love and refused to leave Riga. Tremendous arguments (more like battles) ensued, but I was adamant and could not be persuaded from my decision to marry and delay going to the United States until we both had our visas.

The political situation did not seem dangerous to me, as I perceived the Non-Aggression Pact between Germany and Russia was solid. Finally, the visas to the United States were issued, but the exit visas out of Latvia were difficult to get.

One day my father was called and told that he would receive the exit visa under the following conditions: if he was asked by the Americans how things were in Latvia, he

Drawing of Charlotte by her brother Harry, 1939

was supposed to tell them that everything was very good; he also had to promise them that he would never make any derogatory comments about Latvia or the Russians.

At the same time, he was asked to assist them in a spy operation and was given the following instructions and code: If someone approached him and asked him: "Have we not met in Vienna?" my father should then reply: "No, in Berlin."

My father never became a spy; nobody ever approached him. In March of 1940, my family left Riga for the United

Riga, 1939-1940

States by way of Russia, Manchuria, Japan, and Seattle, Washington. They settled in Port Chester, New York for a short time with my mother's cousin, Fred Wolf, who had sponsored them. It was a difficult trip, made entirely by train, except for the trip from China to Seattle via Japan that took several weeks.

German Occupation, June 1941

After Germany's sudden invasion of the the Soviet Union on June 22, 1941, it took only a few days until the Germans started to bomb Riga. The Russians were not prepared to defend the Baltic states and retreated totally disorganized. There was no question that we wanted to leave Riga; the question was how to accomplish this. Many who attempted to leave returned from the railroad station, as all the trains were already filled. Word of mouth had it that some Jews who used other modes of transportation were apprehended by Latvians and then handed over to the Germans.

All through the night of June 29, the city was bombarded without let up. The house was shaking and we could not decide whether to remain in the apartment or go to the cellar. We compromised and stayed in the entrance hall which gave us quick access to the outside. I sat on a chair and in spite of the unrelenting, terrible sounds of the battle

I sometimes dozed off but always woke up when there was a pause during the shelling.

We lived close to the river and couple of blocks from the very old St Petri church which had very high, slender spire. One time, when we thought that the house was hit, we ran to the door and looked out and what we saw almost paralyzed us: the church had sustained a direct hit and the spire was swaying back and forth, toward the river or us when it finally fell into the river. All through the night the Russians continued to retreat; on June 30, the streets of Riga were deserted except for a few Russian tanks which were supposed to cover the retreating troops. On July 1, 1941, the German army marched into Riga, eagerly awaited and joyously greeted with flowers; the Latvians were jubilant.

By July 16, at least 1000 Jews were killed. Two days before the occupation the Perkonkrust, the Latvian Nazi party, made plans for the destruction of about 40,000 Jews of Riga. The Latvians were recruited by radio and received their white and red armbands and guns. They were assigned their own area of houses out of which they dragged the Jews. They brought them to police headquarters or prison, with accompanying shouting, beatings and brutality of course. Synagogues were burned, but not before the Perkonkrust drove many Jews, men, women and children into the sanctuaries. Buildings were filled to capacities and they even thought up a different twist in atrocities: when the synagogue was filled they forced the overflow of Jews who could not get in, under the muzzles of guns, to put wood and straw around the synagogue, pour kerosene on it and set it on fire. The gang of Latvian fascists, under the able leadership of Victors Arajs, Vilis Hazners, and the dreaded Herbert Cukurs, were responsible for these atrocities and murders of several thousands of Jews in Riga's Central Prison and Riga Police Prefecture.

All this occurred before the German Einsatzgruppe A had a chance to begin their task for the "Final Solution" in Latvia. The Riga Press did its best to fan the hatred of the Latvian populace for the Jews with articles titled "The Jews —Source of our Destruction." An article which was printed on July 11, 1941, ended with the statement that because the Jews had sought to destroy the Latvian nation, they could not be permitted to survive as a national or cultural entity, and therefore all Jews would have to die.

The Jews immediately were forced to work; many worked on construction sites, cleaned the streets of debris, loaded on docks and performed other varied heavy labor. When the German Army arrived in Riga, we frequently worked for them and it was they who would protect us from the brutality of the Latvians. We had to wear a Star of David on our left side and back and were not allowed to walk on the sidewalk. The Latvians plundered Jewish homes, often killing the owners and then moving in.

When a request for workers for a hospital was made, I was fortunate to have been included and was brought to Riga's main hospital which was converted to a military one. My task was to clean 17 rooms that belonged to the doctors and nurses. When the staff realized that I spoke German, I was "promoted" to the "receiving" of wounded from the front whose charts I helped fill out. I continued to the operating room taking dictation during surgery. At least the Wehrmacht (German Army) was decent to us and we received enough food to sustain us. We were allowed to go home in the evening and return next morning.

I developed an infection in my big toe and it became very painful to walk. One of the surgeons noticed my difficulties and offered to lance it.

Somehow, because he seemed kind, I asked him what would become of us and he indicated that eventually we would all be killed. I remember asking him: "Do you mean that we will be stood against the wall and shot?" The answer was in the affirmative. At that time, I absolutely did not believe it! How could anyone order the execution of innocent men, women and children and for the only reason that they were Jews? This was neither imaginable nor comprehensible. How often have I thought of that day when this idea became a reality for thousands of Jews?

Then I finally accepted it, for I realized that we did not deal with humans anymore as we had believed them to be, but with non-humans.

In the beginning of August, thirty or forty Jewish physicians and engineers were released from central prison and there was hope that the thousands who were still incarcerated would also be released. The freed prisoners told their stories: large groups of prisoners were taken somewhere in a continuous flow over a period of many days; none returned.

From information pieced together from inhabitants of

the Bikernieki area we had no doubt that we knew their fate. During the month of July, 1941, many trucks, loaded with people, passed by. Later, uninterrupted firing of machine guns was heard from the direction of the Bikernieki Forest; the trucks returned empty.

The Ghetto

By the middle of August, all Jews were registered in order to determine the number of Jews left after the murders in the streets, prison, and homes. It was then decreed that a ghetto would be established. For this purpose a section of Riga, the "Moscow Suburb" was chosen. It was where Russian workers lived in rather old and dilapidated houses. The poorest of the population had lived here and housing conditions of this area were far inferior to other parts of Riga, many lacking plumbing and electricity. In order to be near their old, beautiful Orthodox churches, most of the Latvians were reluctant to move to better and more comfortable houses (Jewish homes).

At the end, on October 25, 1941 the barbed wire and gates were in place and about 33,000 of us moved into an area which had housed only one third of this number. The streets leading to the ghetto were crowed with masses of Jews moving their belongings into it. We were not allowed to take any large pieces of furniture except beds and took only the most necessary items; the rest we left behind, for we knew that we would have to live in crowded conditions. We were allowed only a specific number of square feet per person. The small apartment we obtained with great difficulties was shared with my cousin Rebecca and two other families.

We were then sealed off, cut off from the outside world, receiving only 50% of the rations of the rest of the population. Signs were posted to the effect that anyone caught too close to the barbed wire would be shot without warning; within a day two women were shot. It was almost impossible not to brush up against the fence; the wire was so close to the narrow sidewalk that it was difficult to keep the required distance.

Work commandos continued to go into the city because their services were requested by the Nazis. Everyone was eager to leave the ghetto, even under guard, hoping to supplement their meager ration. I wound up in a detail that worked in the harbor unloading and sorting vegetables. Other work commandos, not so lucky, were never seen again. Some were transported to the woods after they finished their work and were shot; others returned beaten up. Meanwhile we were hungry; winter had started early and we were cold. There was no firewood; a few trees were felled and then furniture was burned.

And the days passed. We lived under conditions never imagined. Wearing a yellow star on the left chest and one on the back we nevertheless went to various places to work. A "Jewish Committee" was created along with a Jewish police force that was committed to keeping order and facilitating our living under terrible circumstances. The committee also ordered fences behind and between houses to be broken through so that we could reach most places by going through back yards and avoid walking alongside the barbed wire. Work commandos were formed every morning. Requests from various military institutions, including the Gestapo, were filled. We were eager to go out of the ghetto in order to supplement our food, although it became more and more difficult to smuggle anything into the ghetto. Soon meat, herring, and bread was not available anymore. We augmented our meager food ration with provisions we had squirreled away when we first came to the ghetto.

By now we were forbidden to walk on the sidewalk and were forced, outfitted with the double stars, to walk single file in the gutter as we were led to various places of labor. We also got used to nasty and hateful remarks by the local Latvians. Sanitation pick up was forbidden and we were forced to bury garbage and refuse in back yards. Our physicians continued treating us and there were still enough medications stored, for we had lived in the ghetto only for a short time. Little did we know then that this ghetto would only exist for 35 days.

The Ten Bloody Days

On November 27, 1941, a poster informed us that the ghetto would be liquidated and all inhabitants evacuated and resettled. The women, children, and the ones incapable of working would be taken to a special camp. Able bodied men were to remain in the ghetto, in a special fenced area, and would be used for work in the city. The first area to be evacuated was near the ghetto gate. Closed columns of 100 persons each were to be ready on the 29th to start on the journey. They were told to gather in front of their houses and were allowed to take a certain amount of clothing and food. On Friday, November 28th, the last evening that families were together, the ghetto lived through a terrible night knowing that the men would soon be separated from their families. Hopelessness had set in.

At dawn, the able-bodied men were herded together, formed into columns and left to stand for hours in very cold weather. At about one o'clock in the afternoon the order came to move the men into a special area, fenced in by barbed wire inside the ghetto. It was later called the small ghetto. Men were running to say their last good-byes to their loved ones. Everyone thought that it was the men who would be liquidated.

The organization responsible for the liquidation of Jews in Latvia was Einsatzgruppe A. Each of the four Einsatzgruppen had so-called Einsatzkommandos and Sonderkommandos (special details) that took care of the actual executions. They were supported by the Sicherheitsdienst, the Nazi party intelligence service. Einsatzkommando 2C, which was part of Einsatzgruppe A in Riga, was headed by Sturmbannfuehrer Dr. Rudolf Lange. All of a sudden, at about seven o'clock in the evening, thousands of uniformed Latvian SS led by Herbert Cucurs and German SS led by Sturmbannfueher Rudolf Lange, swarmed through the ghetto, broke into houses and chased everyone out, beating and shooting wildly. Children were torn from their mothers' arms and thrown out of windows. Many tried to hide, but these murderers, who stomped through the rooms like wild animals, tore the defenseless victims out of their hiding places and chased them into the streets.

Once outside, the column of young women, women with infants in their arms, old women, handicapped who needed to be assisted, young boys and girls, had to keep moving fast, running sometimes, urged on by shouts of "schnell, schnell" "quickly, quickly," along with beatings and shots. Whips constantly cracked over the heads of the crowd. People trampled over the ones who fell, mowed down by shots. The ill and weak were transported by buses.

The rest were herded toward the gate, the column encircled and guarded by Latvians but led by Germans. This procedure was kept up all night. The streets were covered with blood and the grim task of burying more than 1000 began the next morning. Latvian civilians who lived near the ghetto watched in cold blood, unmoved at what had happened inside the ghetto. Those Jews who remained behind went back to work with their commandos.

Shocked and terrorized, the people were driven in long columns, sometimes almost at a run, heavily guarded by over 15,000 Latvian and German SS, toward the direction of the Rumbuli railroad station and from there to the nearby Rumbuli Forest where Soviet prisoners of war had already dug large mass graves for mass burials. The column started pouring into the forest which was surrounded by a ring of SS men.

Numb with terror, they followed orders mechanically. At the entrance stood a large box, an armed SS man stood next to it and shouted that all valuables and money should be dropped into this box. Then they were driven on a bit further where another Latvian policeman ordered to take their coats off and throw them on top of the pile. One could hear uninterrupted shooting and the prisoners were continually driven on and ordered to take off their clothes, and shoes and drop them at specified locations, while they were running. On they were driven, toward the mass graves, often waiting some time before they too were chased to the edge of the mass graves and shot so that their bodies would fall right into them.

With snow on the ground and in bitter cold, frosty temperature, men, women, and children completely undressed, were not only beaten but many had their gold teeth forcibly removed before being killed. Families tearfully clung together and said their last goodbye. By the thousands, naked, they stood there huddled together, waiting their turn, knowing that they were next. They watched in horror the massacre of their own people, until they too were pushed to the edge of the graves and shot. Many were not even killed when they fell, children were sometimes thrown in alive. A long time afterwards the earth moved. On this night 15,000 were murdered.

Only three women survived this bloodbath. One of them, Frieda Michelson, tried to save herself before being pushed to the edge of the grave. She threw herself to the ground with her face in the snow and lay still, feigning death. She heard somebody saying that there was a dead body on the ground and feared that she too would be dragged to the trench. She heard the screaming of the Jews as they were driven faster and faster, and could hear the trample of their feet, some stepping on her and then, all of sudden, hard objects began falling on her. She finally realized that these were shoes, falling in pairs. She was being covered by them and lays still for many hours in snow and then in a cold puddle of water as the snow melted by her body warmth.

She heard comments made by Latvians of how fine a performance this whole action was, so efficiently organized in the manner the Germans are famous for. She heard a child cry for its mother, the sound coming from the direction of the trench, then shots and all was quiet again.

When there were no more shots for some time, Frieda decided to crawl out from under the pile of shoes toward where she surmised the discarded clothes might be. She found them and when she heard footsteps quickly hid under them and waited. She found some clothes and scarves to fend off the cold and crawled like an animal cautiously through and out of the forest. Later on, when some of us who worked in the city talked to Soviet prisoners, we were told exactly the same story as Frieda Michelson wrote in her book.

The following days were relatively quiet; the ghetto seemed like a ghost town. Nobody ventured out. There were no Germans and all the policemen had disappeared. Gradually, some people started to go out into the streets. The ghetto store opened up again and some differences were noted. Whereas before one could obtain products only by presenting their ration card, now no card was required. There was now more cabbage, beets, carrots and potatoes. People asked questions of each other, analyzed and speculated but had no facts. Where did they take them all? They just could not possibly have killed all of the people in such a short time! The Nazis probably just weeded out the old, sick and infirm. Why would the Germans destroy manpower that could work for them for the cost of below subsistence food rations? Everyone so much wanted to believe that they would be sent to some camp to do work for the Germans.

The remaining Jews of the ghetto were saved for the

time being, and the men in their separate ghetto were able to keep in touch with them. In fact, they were able to go back and forth. At that time, no one suspected the truth about what had happened to the first group after they had left the ghetto. I doubt, had this terrible story been told then, that we would have believed it. The second evacuation started on Monday, December 8, 1941, and the same procedure was repeated. Encircled by Latvian and German SS on foot and horses, these poor victims found their death in the same place and horrible manner as the thousands who were slaughtered the previous week. The trucks again went back and forth and the column marched in the same direction. About 11,500 died that day.

On Tuesday, December 9, 1941, the hunt for the remaining few was on again, and as before, even the most remote hiding place was found and the victims were dragged out and beaten with gun butts and then transported to the Rumbuli Forest. Shortly before 12 p.m., as a new column was just about to be driven to the forest, Jaeger, an SA man, appeared in the ghetto, pulled out his watch and said, "You are lucky! It is one minute after 12, this Action is finished." 500 victims died on this day.

In these ten bloody days, more than 27,000 men, women and children were murdered. The Latvian SS man Herbert Cukurs, and the German SS man Rudolf Lange, were head of the Einsatzkommando (special detail) and responsible for this Action, or "operation." Although Lange supervised the execution, the Latvians actually performed the shooting of the victims only too willingly. Friedrich Yeckeln, who was later executed for wartime crimes, credited the Latvians with strong nerves for executions of this sort, and said that Latvia was the country most conducive to killing Jews. Thus, by December 9, 1941, one of oldest, most distinguished Jewish communities of Eastern Europe was virtually wiped out.

300 Survived

On November 29, rumors surfaced that the Germans were looking for dressmakers and seamstresses to work in the city. I left the apartment trying to find out more about it. I saw a notice posted on a wall with instructions on how to register. It listed the place where the registration would be held. I certainly was not a seamstress, but had been taught to sew leather gloves before I left Berlin. My decision was quickly made. In years to come I would often make snap decisions which would buy me time and save my life. It was mostly instinct and intuition.

I went to the address indicated and found many women there waiting. I was registered without having any difficulties, and remember that about 400 women were registered with me. We were told to go back home to the ghetto, pack food for two days, and then return to the same place at 4 o'clock in the afternoon. From there we would be taken to the city. I went back to the house and consulted with my cousin who also felt that I should take this chance to leave the ghetto. I wrapped some food and also a couple of needles with thread and a pair of tiny manicure scissors which I hid in the hem of my winter coat. I also remembered that I had medication which I needed to take whenever I got one of my frequent sore throats, which always made me acutely ill. I took this along with the food and, after saying goodbye to my cousin, made my way back to where I had previously registered.

Policemen were already waiting for us. It was getting dark and cold as we started to march five abreast. After we crossed almost the entire city and had not arrived at our destination, we became alarmed. Where are they taken us? What will they do with us? Will they shoot us? Then, ending all our speculation, we stopped in front of a great, austere building. We had arrived at the Termin Prison, which housed only women. We were made to wait for some time in the prison yard and then led up to a vast attic. So many people were pushed into this space that there was hardly room to sit. The attic was not heated and there were no sanitary facilities besides a big, open bucket which caused the air to be so foul that it was almost unbearable. We still were apprehensive, not knowing what was in store for us. Still, we were alive at this moment and shared our food with each other. I do not remember much of that night except that I was so exhausted that I occasionally fell asleep for a short period of time only to be awakened by the noise, the light, the cold, and the hard floor. Lice and other insects kept crawling around and the lack of water started bothering us. We all were terribly thirsty.

I do not remember how many days I spent under these conditions and what I remember mostly of that time was an incident that occurred on the second day. At one time, we had to sit in a circle when a German in a military uniform came to inspect us. He walked inside the circle from one woman to another. I was told that he came to a stop in front of me and had stood there for the longest time, staring at me. Everyone was alarmed. I never noticed what was going on and was blissfully unaware of what was happening. I never found out why he singled me out for closer inspection.

Later on in the day a guard came to the door and shouted that there was room for a group of people downstairs and who wanted to volunteer. I did and about fifty of us were taken downstairs to another room which turned out to be just as crowded. Besides, the cement floor was cold and damp. I remember it to be a long, narrow room. At the far end was a small window protected with steel bars. This cell was guarded by a prison guard. This night, too, passed and we were as uncomfortable as during the previous ones, huddled together on the cold cement floor. The next day the prison supervisor came in and ordered us to give him a "report." We did not understand what he wanted and asked for clarification. This infuriated him to such a degree that he started to scream at us. I do not remember exactly what he said but knew that in effect he was cursing us.

Another day passed. The physical and mental atmosphere and the uncertainty all added to break our spirits, and our hopes to be released were dashed. Suddenly, the door opened and the supervisor appeared, shouting that we all had to leave this cell immediately. We all panicked thinking that we were going to be shot. We were brought to the prison yard and ordered to form a column, then were led into another building into an area which looked like a large corridor. At the end of this room, at tables near some windows, sat Germans in military uniform. They were sorting the women, some to the right and others to the left. One group was designated as seamstresses, the others were to be sent back to the ghetto. When my turn came, I was asked a few questions, I do not remember what exactly they were, but my answer apparently qualified me to be put in the group of seamstresses. I remained with this group until the selection was finished and all women were either in the group on the left or right. The smaller group was led out the building and, what we perceived at that time, to their freedom. We lamented the fact that our group of 300 women was kept in prison. Why could not we also leave this horrible place? None of us believed in the story that we were needed as seamstresses.

Our group was led back to the other building and brought back to the cells we had occupied previously. I do not remember much of the next few days as, what I feared most, came to pass: I came down with an extremely painful sore throat and high fever. All I remember was that I was lying on the cold, damp cement floor wrapped in my coat. I had this medicine, which I believe must have been sulfur, and I swallowed the pills at intervals. The pain to swallow anything was sheer agony. As a teenager I had been plagued with this malady and this was the first time that I had not the tender care of my family. How miserable I was, shivering with cold which kept me from sleeping for more than a few minutes at a time. And so we passed another few days in utter misery.

On or around December 11, 1941, I believe, we were told that we were going to leave the prison. Grouped in a column, 300 women were again marched through the streets of Riga. To our surprise, we were led back to the ghetto. To our horror, we saw that the ghetto was totally deserted and devoid of any life. The streets were littered with packages, bags, items of clothing. It was a frosty, crystal clear day. The sun was shining, the sky very blue and the only sound heard was the sound of our footsteps. We were led past the barbed wire which enclosed the section where the men who had survived the massacre, were housed. Along the entire fence they stood, watching us, trying to find any of their loved ones. There were about 3000 men in the ghetto at that time. Shouts of joy, though too few, punctuated the air when someone saw a familiar face. Agony and grief showed in the faces of the men whose last hope was dashed when we told them that we were the only women survivors of what was then called the "ten bloody days." The women who had been released from prison earlier had been led back to the ghetto in time to be taken with the last Aktion and were executed in the forest.

We stopped at a housing complex on Ludzas and Liksnas near what was called the "little ghetto" where the men were housed. The house was isolated and fenced in by barbed wire. This was to be our "home." So, all that was left of the 32,000 people who had lived in the ghetto at the end of November were the 3000 men, 300 women from prison, and a few women and some children who were able to hide themselves successfully during the round-up. We were still shocked and stunned from our stay in prison and our release suddenly into the empty ghetto. A story circulated that one SS man, knowing the fate of all women, made a last-ditch effort to save some and therefore was responsible for the internment of the women in prison. On the other hand, there may have been a need for a female labor force. At any rate, there may have been a need for skilled labor for the military and also for the SS. The military complained that the Aktion had cut into the labor force and could not be replaced since the local Gentile population was not trained to take the place of those who were killed.

This need for workers helped prolong the lives of the Jewish deportees from the Reich who had begun to arrive in Riga on December 12, 1941. Those transports were never supposed to have arrived in Riga but were to have been brought to Salaspils and Jungfernhof, two concentration camps built for the purpose of being used as transit camps. The Jews were there to stay for only as long as it would take to eliminate the majority of inmates. There would be "selections." The inmates would line up and the same procedure would follow as the one in prison. Those classified as fit to work would be ordered to move to one side, usually to the right. Those unfit for work were told to move to the other side and subsequently would be exterminated. The victims were hauled off in trucks to the already dug out graves in the forest. Children and people over 50 were usually the first to be categorized as unfit.

Salaspils was more than one hour away from the city and from the war plants and army bases which had requested workers; therefore Dr. Lange decided to bring later transports to the original ghetto and have them move into the houses left vacant by the Latvian Jews who had been killed. Starting on December 10, 1941, the first transport from the Reich began to arrive in Riga. Eventually, twenty transports, totaling 20,057 Jews from different towns of Germany, Austria and Czechoslovakia reached Riga. Then, on February 5, 1942, through another selection which Dr. Lange conducted in the German ghetto, more than 2000 Jews lost their lives in the forest as their Latvian counterparts had previously. A few days later a similar "operation" was conducted in Jungfernhof and about 1,000 Jews were taken to their deaths.

As of February 10, 1942, there were 2,500 Jews in Jungfernhof, 11,000 Jews in the German ghetto, 3,000 men and 300 women in the Latvian ghetto, and 1,300 men in Salaspils. Salaspils had the highest death rate of all the labor camps. It was estimated that about 80% of all inmates perished and new groups of men were constantly taken from the German ghetto to replenish the labor force.

When on December 10 the first German transports arrived in the ghetto, they found the houses in terrible disarray. Clothes, linen and household utensils were strewn all over the rooms. Blood stains were to be found in the rooms and outside. There still was food, frozen solid, on the tables, evidence of the hasty departure of the occupants. Only certain houses were available to the newly arrived transports. Others were strictly off limits, as the SS had not completed their thorough search for jewelry, money, and furs. The German ghetto was separated from ours, the Latvian, by barbed wire. The streets, originally named in Latvian, were renamed by the name of the town where the transportees originated. Therefore, there was a Berliner Street, a Hannover Street, etc.

The two ghettos were strictly segregated and the only time contact was made was when they met outside the ghetto where they were performing some work for the Germans. Then the prisoners were able to talk to each other and exchange information. There was resentment toward the German Jews as the Latvian Jews assumed that the Latvian women and children were killed in order to provide housing for the transports out of the Reich. The inmates of the German ghetto thought that they might be safe as they, being German speaking, would receive preferential treatment. Needless to say, both assumptions proved to be completely erroneous.

There was one surprise in store for me when I received a note which was smuggled to our women's ghetto. It was from Inge, my best friend from Berlin. Her transport from Berlin had arrived in Riga on January 16, 1941. The last time we saw each other was on January 29, 1939, when we were leaving Berlin to go to Riga. She came to the train station to see us off. I still remember that she brought a bar of chocolate. Although most people in transports from the Reich reached Riga with their families, Inge came alone, as her parents and brother were sent to Auschwitz. Even under the most crowded conditions, these deportees led their own family life. Religious life was observed and schools for children of all ages were started.

The ghetto was ruled by SS Obersturmfuehrer Krause, aided in all murderous undertaking by the Latvian guards who were headed by Danskop and the murderers Tuchel, Neuman, and Robiello. Among others, they were responsible for many deaths of inmates of the ghetto.

The women who returned from prison, the few who had hidden with their children, and later on, several more from Kowno, Lithuania, occupied an apartment complex. Many of us lived in one room. It was very crowded. Still, how much better this was than what we came from. We found some wood and were able to keep warm. There still was some food left from the previous owners who were driven away to their deaths. We were all in a state of shock from all that had happened to us in so short a time, trying to cope with our grief at the realization of what must have happened to our relatives.

Except for one of the girls, Jenny, I cannot remember the others who were in our room. We all were getting along; we were still "civilized". Jenny's husband lived in the men's ghetto and was one of the lucky ones whose wife had returned from the Termin prison. She already was in the early stages of pregnancy. She later gave birth and when at a future action the baby was selected, Jenny and her husband chose to go together with the baby in the truck which took all of them to their deaths.

I found it difficult to sleep. The bedbugs drove me nearly crazy. I have forgotten much, but I still remember jumping out bed one time and counting the bites - 63 of them! I must have been particularly sensitive to them. As soon as the weather permitted, I pulled the bed apart and brought it piece by piece into the courtyard and poured hot water into every crevice.

The winter of 1941-42 was one of the harshest ever to be remembered. It was bitter cold, near minus 40 degrees at times. This cold, coupled with meager rations, brought great hardship. To make our situation even harder to bear, we were required to hand over warm coats and furs. The supply of wood for heating diminished and soon there was great need for it. Everybody tried to obtain even one piece of wood and smuggle it into the ghetto. The price of getting caught smuggling anything, be it a potato or a piece of wood, was death. The execution proceeded immediately. The victim was hauled to the old Jewish cemetery which was located nearby, placed against the wall and shot by Krause himself. Others, not so fortunate, were hanged.

As the ghetto was void of women, work which was customarily done by them was now done by men. This changed as soon as the women were released from prison. By that time, a police headquarters for the guards and a Kommandantur (command post) was established. They were housed just a block away from the women's ghetto. The Kommandantur housed both the central office for work administration and the offices of the commandant of the ghetto. As luck willed it, I was recruited to work at the Kommandantur. Apparently, there was a need for workers who spoke German. There were several of us; we cleaned and cooked.

One girl, who used to work as a secretary, became Krause's private secretary. I do remember having cooked Russian beet soup fairly often as this soup was a favorite of the Germans. Naturally, I was most fortunate to have found myself in the "lion's den," for I was warm and able to supplement my ration. We all kept a low profile, hoping not to provoke Krause, as we knew fully well what he was capable of.

Still, the horror of our situation was brought back to me daily when, looking out of the window, I was able to watch the work commandos who worked in the city return to the ghetto. Everyone became adept at hiding and smuggling a little bit of food or firewood into the ghetto, fully well knowing what the punishment would be if caught. The chance to be caught when Krause was bloodthirsty and initiated a search was greatest when the first column returned to the ghetto. The succeeding groups then knew what was waiting for them and relieved themselves of every item they tried to bring in. They threw everything away before passing through the gate.

To assist in the smooth running of the ghetto, the Germans relied on the Jewish police and men who supervised work details. In the women's ghetto a few women were active as police women, who supervised the work force and made sure that the sanitary conditions were kept up. We also maintained a small room used as a hospital room. Abortions were performed as giving birth was punishable by death. Another baby was born, named Ben Ghetto, son of the ghetto. He and his parents went to their death with another selection.

Good organization allowed both ghettos to function as best as was possible under conditions no one ever had experienced before. Announcements or orders from the Nazi authorities were conveyed to the ghetto inmates through the central ghetto administration. Everyone active in ghetto administration was dedicated to work with one thought; to make life easier for all of us.

Despair

L ife went on. Winter passed, I had survived the first winter. The snow melted and weather became warmer, making life a bit more bearable. There was a constant request for workers. The city kept requesting people for railroads, harbor, army barracks, construction, etc. Private and military facilities needed workers and the ghetto inmates were only too happy to oblige.

The requesting private firms or military installations sent their foreman to the ghetto with a request for laborers, took them away and then brought them back at night. There was always a group leader among us who took responsibility for organization and communication of that particular labor detail. Later on, some of the workplaces found it more expedient to keep their group in place and created housing for them. Everyone tried to find themselves such a situation, for it was much safer than to return to the ghetto.

There were constantly incidents which made us despair even more. One evening, an order came that all Latvian men had to proceed in closed columns and hand over any cash or valuables still in their possession. Anything found after this would be punishable by death. Everything collected was given to Kommandant Krause who seemed very pleased when he was able to retain a lot of the collection for himself.

When in March of 1942 the German authorities deemed the German ghetto overcrowded, they decreed the necessity of a "resettlement" to Dünamünde. There, they said, was a need for workers in fish canneries. This plan sounded credible as the Baltic Sea was rich in fish. For this sinister purpose, the ghetto administration was ordered to turn over to the Kommandantur certain quotas of people. Men and women in charge of labor detail administration had to compile lists of names. Mostly the elderly or ailing and parents with small children were chosen, but also some physicians and a few from the ghetto administration. All were willing as they hoped that the new camp would provide more food and easier living conditions.

The ghetto lost 1900 Jews on March 15, 1942. There was no town called "Dünamünde." It all was a ruse. The inventor of this deception, Gerhard Maywald, boasted of it during his trial in 1977. There was no doubt at all of the fate of the transport selected. This massacre was supervised by Kurt Krause and, as in previous cases, the Latvians brutally shot the victims in the Bikernieki Forest. Two days later trucks drove into the ghetto and were unloaded. The cargo contained clothes, taken off hurriedly, still turned inside out, muddy shoes, children's toys, bags with food and documents. The women who were forced to sort all items from the truck before these were sent to Germany found identity cards and, of course, recognized the clothes which their friends and neighbors wore when they left the ghetto.

Krause and Rudolf Lange roamed around the ghetto and, if in a bad mood, would find some obscure reason to beat or shoot someone. Constant Aktions and subsequent killings made all of us despondent. If one person fled, three were taken hostages and shot at the cemetery wall. We all were aware that transports which came to Riga and neighboring towns were exterminated. Ghetto inmates who worked in the city were given a continuous flow of clothing and jewelry to sort out. During this process they found names and addresses on suitcases, and were able to tell where these transports had originated.

We drew some hope again when we heard that the United States, Britain, the Soviet Union and China had joined forces. Surely Germany could not hold out long against such massive strength and as long as they needed our labor force, we stood a chance to survive.

I continued to be brought to the city for various kinds of work of short duration. Every night we were led back to the house and room I shared with other women. My roommates essentially remained the same. Of course, I always dreaded to come back, not knowing what terrible things might have occurred during our absence. Sometime in the spring of 1942 I was brought to Riga's largest hotel, Hotel Rom. There the work for women consisted of various kitchen duties and cleaning rooms; for the men, transport, carpentry, etc. This work commando was one of the best, for it provided a possibility of obtaining some food to add to our meager rations we were allotted in the ghetto. The ratio, 220 grams of bread per day, occasionally some turnips, cabbage or potatoes, all in various degree of decay, and from time to time, one portion of horse meat or not so fresh fish, never stilled our hunger. Although when I first tasted horse meat I shook with disgust, I was so hungry that I could not get enough of it.

Only the military occupied Hotel Rom where about 3000 meals per day were served. All day I sat with several women and peeled potatoes; hour after hour, bucket after bucket. As soon as one was filled, it was brought to the kitchen. There were no potato peelers and we became very proficient at this task; to this very day, my family marvels at how fast and thinly I peel potatoes and apples. We really tried to do a good job for we wanted to be needed in order to stay with this commando. When the manager of a workplace decided that it would be more expedient to house their workers on their premises, permission usually was granted. Our foreman requested to have us remain in the city, citing convenience as the reason, for some of us worked in shifts.

To our great joy, permission was granted. This provided for us a safer and better environment to live in. Some of our men with knowledge of carpentry built some bunks and so we were housed in an annex to the hotel. We also were allowed to cook our own food as the ghetto still supplied our rations. Food was now more substantial as a few potatoes were hardly missed and with a quick hand, when passing by a kettle of soup stock, I was able to scoop up a cup of this nourishing broth. During the night shift, when there was hardly anyone in the kitchen, I was able to "organize" enough for all of us. We never were without a small cup, which we kept hidden, should an opportunity present itself to supplement our rations. We all became magicians; our dexterity to make food vanish out of the kitchen surpassed that of any professional. Houdini could not have done better!

Of course, taking anything from the Germans was never called stealing. We used the word "organize" and applied it liberally to describe the act of getting what was rightfully ours. We organized food, wood, clothing, etc. This act could be called one of form of resistance. I think that we protected ourselves from the knowledge that we were reduced to stealing in order to stay alive a little longer by calling it "organizing."

The kitchen was gigantic and so was the soup stock pot which I estimated to be at least two feet high. A great quantity of bones were thrown into the pot, covered with water and let to simmer all night; the resulting broth was high in protein and when cooled could almost be cut with a knife. How fortunate for us; we had a reprieve from starvation! Not only that, but we also were able to build up our bodies so, when back on starvation diet, we were able to hold out longer. We now worked in three shifts.

The women either peeled potatoes or other vegetables, cleaned or washed dishes. The dining rooms were immense, with windows reaching up to the ceiling so that I needed a tall ladder to wash them. Once I fell off a ladder and landed on top of the pail I was using. The pail was full of water and the rim dug into my ribs and cracked some. It was sheer agony to breathe and I was made more comfortable when strips of old sheets were wound around my sore ribs. Needless to say, I continued to work. When dishes needed to be washed it seemed to me that there was no end to it and truly there never was. Hour after hour, stack after stack, there was no reprieve. They kept coming and I was afraid that if I was not fast enough, they would pile on top of me. No wonder that I turned out to be such an efficient housekeeper--did I not get a lot of experience during this time?

Every day we hoped that we would continue to stay here; we were treated decently, although considered prisoners. After we were finished with work, we were allowed to go to our quarters to sleep and also to cook our meals.

The "organized" food came in handy, for we were truly most inventive to come up with new recipes. We used potato peels in all of our cooking and came up with a pseudo chopped liver made with yeast. We knew that we were lucky to be at this place and dreaded the day when we would have to leave. We knew that nothing had changed in the ghetto and the inmates were still exposed to being terrorized by Krause and his henchmen.

The dreaded day finally arrived and we were all brought back to the ghetto and I went back to the women's small ghetto where I had lived before. This probably occurred in early fall of 1942. I remember an incident on October 31, 1942, which completely shocked us. To this very day I still remember the horror I felt on hearing that our entire Latvian Jewish Police were marched to the Tin Square and machine-gunned down. Forty-one of the finest young men were killed that day. The reason for the shooting was that an arsenal of guns was found hidden in the Latvian ghetto and it was assumed that an uprising was planned. A list implicating a few of the policemen was found but the Germans assumed that it would be wiser to kill the entire police force. Later on it turned out that several small groups had been formed and had discussed secret plans of an armed resistance. The men had not forgotten the bloody days in November and December of 1941. Many members of the police force were taken into their confidence. There had been many theories proposed of how the Germans ever found the place in which the guns were hidden. It is possible that not one single discovery was responsible. It was rumored that a list with names was found and ensuing occurrences led to the discovery of the cash. Among several theories, it was mentioned that a man who had fled the ghetto was caught and broke down after being interrogated under torture.

Winter

The second winter began and with it a change. Kommandant Krause was transferred and was replaced by Obersturmfuehrer Eduard Roschmann, a lawyer from Graz, Austria. He continued in the same vein as his predecessor, Krause. He walked through the ghetto in the company of his assistant, Gimmlich, and his dangerous dog. He would, at a whim, make a surprise visit to homes, looking into pots in which food was cooking. As soon as it is was apparent that he was starting to walk through the streets of the ghetto, food which was illegally obtained with great effort was thrown away. He also visited the hospital in order to check if all the people there were really "legally" excused. Toward evening, one could find him and Gimmlich at the gate. When the returning work commandos neared the gate and saw from afar that Roschmann and his assistant were present, they threw away anything they might have obtained in the way of food. If something would have been found on them, they would have been brought to the Bunker, the holding cell, and from there to the cemetery wall to be executed. Later, the food was gathered by the Jewish ghetto police and distributed to the Jewish administration. Firewood, as well as food, was a precious commodity to be smuggled into the ghetto.

Roschmann, by the way, figures prominently in the plot of the 1972 novel, *The Odessa File*, by John Forsyth.

Although the prospect of spending another cold winter in the ghetto with not enough food was unthinkable, the consolation was that our lives would be temporarily spared because the city still experienced an acute labor shortage. Meanwhile, I had been working in different outside commandos, but coming back to the ghetto every night hoping that I would get lucky and find a commando which would be housed at the place of work. Everyone's goal was to leave the ghetto. When more seamstresses were requested, I was at the right place at the right time, and was put into a commando which turned out to be none other than the one that did work for the Gestapo.

The idea of working for the Gestapo, the most feared department of the Nazis, scared me at the beginning. I was very relieved when I found myself in the "lions den." The Gestapo man, Scherwitz, who was in charge of us, treated us decently and arranged for the group to stay on and not to return to the ghetto at night. This was by far the best "Kasernierung" as this was called when commandos lived in the place where they worked.

When, after the liquidation of our ghetto, this facility was moved across the Duna river and housed in the Lenta factory, it was renamed SD Werkstaette Lenta (Lenta Security Service Repair Shop). As manager of this department, Boris Rudow, a well-known tailor from Riga, was installed to oversee the Jews who worked under him. He had gained the confidence of Scherwitz so that he was exempted from wearing the Star of David. In a short time, he received papers which claimed that he was of Aryan decent but had been adopted by Jews. He was a kind man and was able, because of his position, to help his less fortunate brothers.

Most men did physical labor; the women cleaned; or, as in my case, were sewing on machines which were set up in large rooms. Military uniforms were sent from the front, cleaned and then given to us to be mended. The work consisted of mostly patching holes with material cut up from uniforms which were beyond repair. After the uniforms were repaired, they would be sent back. There were also furriers at work, for it was winter and furs were needed at the front.

We slept in rooms in which bunk beds were set up. Men and women were segregated, but we were still in communication with each other. We were warm. There were some opportunities to supplement our rations. Best of all, we were away from the ghetto. In February, 1943, when the German army suffered a great defeat at the Eastern front, our hopes were fanned again. Could we be saved after all? Could freedom be just around the corner?

Little did we know at that time that our fate had already been decided. Early in 1943, SS Chief Heinrich Himmler had made plans to do away with the entire ghetto system that had been set up in the East and build concentration camps nearby. The large-scale uprising in the Warsaw Ghetto might have been a contributing factor, but we never even had heard about the liquidation of this or other ghettos in Poland.

The site selected was found in the Riga suburb called Mezapark. Camp Kaiserwald was being built with the idea of bringing together the Jews from the two Riga Ghettos, as well as all those from all "outside" labor details, who had been living at their places of work. Kaiserwald was started in March, 1943, and built by 500 non-Jewish prisoners from the Sachsenhausen concentration camp under such severe conditions that when the Jews from the ghetto started to arrive, there were only 300 still living. For that reason, our prison numbers started with 501. Around July, 1943, the first transport to Kaiserwald began. It was known that only the strongest and healthiest individuals would be transferred to the new camp and again an Aktion was initiated. On November 1, 1943, 2500 women, children, older and weak looking Ghetto inmates were selected and trucked to their death.

In command was the SS man *Obersturmbannführer* Albert Sauer, who selected murderers like himself to assist him. The ones I remember among the most vicious was an SS man Sorge, nicknamed "The Iron Gustav," for he was famous for shooting his victims in the neck, Wiesner, Dr. Krebsbach and, unsurpassed in brutality, the SS woman Kova. To understand how the camp was run, I will just say that outside of a few SS men, the most important posts in the camp were filled from the ranks of criminals, murderers, thieves, pimps and prostitutes and a few political prisoners. These "professional criminals" were Gentiles who were serving prison terms at the camp.

The prisoner in charge at the beginning was Reinhold Rosenmeyer, a political prisoner, who in time became more lenient and tried to ease our almost intolerable condition. Most likely, his treatment of the Jews may have been too humane in the eyes of the SS so that later he was transferred to the nearby camp, Strassenhof, and replaced by another prisoner, Hans Brunns, who had had the position of senior overseer there and had treated the Jewish inmates brutally and sadistically. We all were unhappy to see Rosenmeyer leave our camp. Besides the German prisoners who became our overseers, there were about 70 gentile prisoners, mostly Poles and Ukrainians, who committed numerous acts of brutalities and killed many Jews. The political prisoners, in contrast to the rest of the assorted criminals, treated us more humanely.

Next in importance to Rosenmeyer was a professional criminal brutalizing the camp. He was called Mister X. His real name was Xavier Abel. He was a handsome man, always impeccably dressed in a navy blue suit with gray stripes, a blue, round hat, similar to a navy hat, and high leather boots. Because of those stripes we called them "Zebras." Mr. X was known as an international con man and car thief. Everyone in the camp trembled when he appeared. No one would know when it might be his or her turn to be the recipient of his brutality for no apparent reason. He would walk through the camp, past some unsuspecting, unfortunate inmate and before one knew, delivered some devastating blows which rendered his defenseless victim into a heap on the ground. These beatings were mostly reserved for the men; the women would receive a slap in the face for anything he would deem an offense.

Kaiserwald was divided into three divisions: the administrative, the men's and women's camps. At the entrance of the former was a large barracks for the guards who counted the inmates when they returned from work outside the camp. The living quarters of the SS commander and his assistants, and the SS kitchen and quarters for the guards could also be found in this part of the camp. There also was a large barracks that was used to store and sort the clothing collected when transports arrived at the camp. Many Jewish women and men worked there. Valuables and good clothing was taken by the SS and sent to their relatives in Germany. The women's and men's camps were divided by two rows of barbed wire fence with about two yards in between them. There were times when women and men were able to communicate through the fence, but this pleasant interlude would end as soon as the guards would see us talking to each other. They would start to beat us and we quickly ran from the fence to our barracks.

The various categories of prisoners were forced to wear triangles of different colors next to their numbers. Criminals wore green triangles; Jews were identified by yellow, political prisoner by red, and prostitutes by a black triangle. Some were marked by the letters B.V. which stood for professional criminal (Berufsverbrecher).

We knew that in July, 1943, the first transport left the ghetto to be transferred to Kaiserwald and that by the end of October, most inmates had been sent out of the ghetto. On November 2, 1943, a few remaining labor details left the ghetto and went to work. The only people left in the ghetto were old people, children and their teachers. Also remaining were the sick. Many of those had been returned disabled from Kaiserwald to recover in the ghetto hospital and would have been sent back to the camp once they recovered. When the work commandos returned to the ghetto they found that all who had remained there that morning had been taken away. It was estimated that between 2,000 and 2,500 had been transported to Auschwitz.

Theoretically, all Jews working in and around Riga belonged to Kaiserwald. Anyone who was living at a facility outside the camp, and became ill and unable to work would be returned to Kaiserwald to "recuperate". The barracks, which housed the sick and moribund was called the Lazarett, and served only as a facility which accommodated prisoners unable to work. Therefore they were exempted from standing for roll call and work. There were no medications to treat the illnesses most prevalent at that time: primarily, dysentery, typhus and of course, the ravages of starvation. In command of these facilities were the camp physician SS-Sturmbannfuehrer Dr. Krebsbach and his assistant, SS-Oberscharfuehrer Wiesner.

The supervision and responsibility for the ill inmates and the administration of the "Lazarett" was assumed by the medical staff of Jewish inmates which was comprised of doctors and nurses. Of course, they could do little to alleviate the suffering except for their caring attitude, and by sometimes defying orders from the SS. In one instance, for example, the medical staff was required to notify the SS of all sick inmates who were there for more than 21 days. That was the allotted number of days that a prisoner was allowed to spend in this facility.

At times, the staff was able to change the date of their being admitted and so helped to save them. Actions occurred often when all the sick people were taken out of the Lazarett. We did not know where they were transported to, as no one had ever returned. We surmised that this was what was called Himmelfahrtskommando, loosely translated, "skyride commando," when the weak and ill were removed from the camp. The implication, of course, was certain death for those inmates.

I was still working in Lenta and hoping that I would be spared being sent to Kaiserwald, for I already had heard gruesome details about life there, but my turn came in the fall of 1943. I do not remember whether our group returned first to the ghetto or were transported directly to the camp. What I do remember is the panic, the sheer terror at arriving in a truck at the camp where we were "greeted" by our overseers with beating, kicking and shouting and being pushed through the gate.

We were brought to one of the barracks and made to stand there. During this time our few meager possessions were taken away. The shouting never stopped as we were herded toward another barracks, the showers, which comprised three rooms. In the first room we had to strip in front of the SS and suffer the indignation of being examined for lice. At that time, we had not acquired any, although that would change in a short time.

We were then herded into the showers where one either got scalded with too hot water or shivered under too cold one. Then we were chased, dripping wet as there were no towels, to another room. Pieces of clothing, often mere rags, were thrown at us. Regardless whether they fit us or not, we had to dress ourselves in them. What a sight we made! We looked like scarecrows. The tall women got clothes too short for them and the short ones practically fell out of theirs. Throughout this whole procedure our overseers never stopped yelling, berating and beating us.

We finally were led into our barracks. We all were totally terrorized, a feeling that would not leave us for the duration of our stay in Kaiserwald. By now, it was quite late in the evening and we had not eaten. Nobody knew what we were waiting for. We stood around wondering what was in store for us. Time passed and there was no evidence that our food ration for the day would ever be distributed. It must have been close to midnight and we all gave up hope of getting some food when we were ordered by the elder of the barracks to form a line so that we could receive our ration of bread, 200-250 grams of heavy bread. It felt so dense that many were of the opinion that part of it was made by adding sawdust to it.

We were then assigned to our "beds", which consisted of shelves in two tiers, an upper and a lower bunk that stretched almost from one end of the room to the other. Each of us was allowed a sack filled with straw which served as a mattress. The straw kept falling to the lower bunk making the women trying to sleep there miserable. For this reason, we always tried to occupy the upper bunk. Exhaustion overtook us and we slept for just minutes it seemed to me, when a shrill whistle woke us. The day in Kaiserwald began at 4 o'clock in the morning. Again we were screamed at as we were chased out of our bunks and allowed to go to the washroom. There, over metal troughs, horizontal pipes dripped water. Back in the barracks we each received "coffee" poured into a bowl. Most of us had learned to ration our piece of bread so that we had something for the next morning. We also learned never to separate from our little crust of bread. It was always with us; we even slept on top of it; we guarded it, for it was our lifeline. When hunger gnawed at our insides we did not tempt others by leaving food around; I had to fight constantly the impulse to eat all my bread the moment I received it.

Soon, a bell rang; time for the morning Appell. We had to stand five in a row to be counted. In heat, in cold, in rain or snow, we had to stand. One could be sick unto death, and still have to go out there to be counted. To be found in the barracks would call for severe punishment. On a good day, when the number tallied at the first call, we were allowed to return to our barracks after a relatively short time.

There would be times when the count did not tally immediately and would be repeated over and over again, regardless if it were raining or snowing, soaking us to the skin. The weaker ones would fall to the ground; still the roll call would be continued until the number tallied. This procedure was repeated at least twice a day, and I later learned it was common to all concentration camps. It was dreaded by all prisoners, as one never knew what might befall an inmate during this time. I do not remember whether I was registered on the first night or the following morning. At any rate I ceased to have a name and became a prisoner with a number. The individual numbers were painted on a little piece of cloth which, with a yellow triangle, we had to wear on our clothes.

In addition to our ration of coffee, bread, and margarine in the evening, we received watery beet or cabbage soup for lunch. To find a piece of vegetable or potato was considered extraordinary luck. On Sundays our ration sometimes included a tablespoon of sugar. Those rations were hardly sufficient to sustain us; to continue working without breaking down was really out of the question. Anyone lucky enough to have been in a labor detail outside the camp stood at least a chance to sometimes acquire some additional food. A few potatoes, an extra piece of bread, a pat of margarine, anything edible would keep us a little longer from starvation and illness. Although we had, by this time, plenty of practice how to hide illegal acquisitions, there were still instances when someone was unfortunate and got caught. A special barracks reserved for punishment without food was the mildest form of punishment; otherwise beatings were in order.

Quite a few inmates were put to work inside the camp, in the kitchen or in a special barracks where clothes, which were taken away from new arrivals, were sorted. Even prisoners with special mechanical background were used. Shoemakers, seamstresses and tailors were needed and put to work in the camp. I was put to work in a commando of women called Anoden, meaning battery anodes. We went to another barracks where we took apart old and damaged telephones and telegraph equipment. I recall vaguely using a hammer to demolish some items and saving others, most likely the anodes in the vacuum tubes. We were covered from head to toe with the exuded black dust and dirt. At noon, when the bell rang we were rushed outside to stand in a long line in order to receive our watery soup.

The weather turned colder and we were not adequately

dressed for winter. Constant selections and exterminations, the overpowering feeling of terror, hunger and cold, coupled with extreme humiliation, broke the spirits of many and ended their hope of survival. Coats finally were distributed, but the results of the delay and malnutrition were that many died in the winter of 1943. The harassments by the "Zebras" never ended. We could always count on beatings during the coming and going of the labor details, during the endless roll calls, and just having the misfortune of crossing their paths.

My morale was low already. This was the third winter and there was no end in sight. But this was nothing compared with how I felt when I discovered lice on my body! I was utterly degraded and revulsed. Now I, too, joined the ranks of women examining their bodies and clothes for lice. We devoted every free minute of our time to this task. In the evening, practically all of the women were sitting in their bunks occupied with getting rid of these pests by picking them off their bodies and clothes and killing them. This was accomplished by cracking them to death between the nails of the thumbs. As these pests hid in the seams of our clothes and laid eggs, this was a never ending fight. Of course, because of the unsanitary conditions, disease was rampant, typhus in particular. The chances to recover, living under the conditions found in Kaiserwald, were very slim. The only hope one had to survive Kaiserwald was to go on a labor detail outside the camp where there might be a chance to obtain extra food and to work in a building sheltered from the elements.

Kaiserwald

I was most fortunate that winter that I was not sent on a snow removing detail which worked for the military in the city. Several transports arrived at Kaiserwald; some came from Latvian towns; others from Poland. One transport arrived from the Vilna ghetto after it had been liquidated. Several women were assigned to the barracks in which I stayed. One of the girls, Feige, had a beautiful voice and sang sad and haunting ghetto songs. Those songs were composed out of feelings of despair, suffering and agony. Some of these songs have been preserved and are still sung at special occasions. Feige suffered frequent, painful episodes which we thought were gallbladder attacks. Of course, not having access to any medications, the poor girl suffered tormenting pain.

In 1970 or 1971, when I took my mother, who had moved to California, to San Francisco to purchase various kosher products and meat, we stopped at a shop on Geary Avenue. During the time she was selecting different items, I struck up a conversation with a man who worked in the shop. When I found out that he came from Vilna, I mentioned that I had known a girl who came from there to our concentration camp. Well, his wife, too, came from Vilna. I then remarked about the beautiful voice of hers and he replied that his wife, also, sings well. I then told him her name, and sure she, too, was called Feige. When I mentioned her painful attacks, he said that those were caused by ulcers. It was the same Feige who had given us beautiful interludes with her singing. I subsequently visited her.

A Change of Seasons and of Life

Harassment by the professional prisoners at Kaiserwald continued and one would never know, when walking from one barracks to another, that a person might be unfortunate enough to pass one of the professionals who just happened to feel like beating a Jewish prisoner. One incident occurred which I believe must have been divine intervention, although at that time I did not know it. Mr. X continued his brutal treatment of prisoners most of the time; still there were times when he was in a good mood, and would astonish some prisoners by just talking to them.

After one of the usual roll calls Mr. X mentioned that he came from Berlin and inquired if anyone else came from there. I told him that I too came from there, and when he asked which part of town we lived, I also mentioned that we had owned the restaurant Eszterhazy Keller on Friedrich Strasse. He knew it, he said; he had been there, and I felt horror that such a person could have been in our restaurant. But then, it could have been possible, for the business was open 18 to 20 hours a day and frequented by different strata of society. It was located in the center of town and easily reached by various forms of transportation. From then on, whenever meeting me, he would call out: "Hello, Berlin!" and at times would make some conversation. I must admit that from then on I felt a little safer, believing that he would not pose any threat to me.

As the winter of 1943 continued, our hope diminished. Many more inmates from other camps who took ill and did not recover within a certain time were transported back to Kaiserwald. When they did not recover promptly, they would be exposed to the danger of one of the many selections and subsequent transport to certain death. All of us yearned to leave this camp and to be housed in some other installation where treatment might be more humane. There was A.B.A., Armeebekleidungsamt (army clothing supply center) which was located outside of Riga, and had close to 2000 Jews working there. Conditions there were a little better, but not by very much. A labor detail which treated the prisoners a little better was the Feldbekleidngsamt der Luftwaffe (clothing supply office for the air force).

In January 1944, I was added to the detail which worked for the military. It was called H.K.P., short for Heereskraftfahrpark, a military vehicle park. The men worked as mechanics repairing vehicles, and as plumbers, radio repairmen, painters, tailors and carpenters. The women mostly cleaned and washed. We were housed in recently built barracks. We slept in double bunks which also had been newly built. They were closely spaced; but how grateful we were that they were so clean. Life improved. I was fortunate, as this was the best place to be under the circumstances. Of course, we were still supervised by Kaiserwald and received our rations from there, but we were not guarded except when we were led to departments outside this facility. In short, we were self-governing and our commando leader, Max Kaufmann, was made responsible for us. We were constantly counted to be sure that no one had left the premises.

When we were ill, we were assisted by our own physician and were allowed to stay in our barracks. At that time I developed painful boils, mostly on my back but some on one leg. They were carbuncles, probably caused by a staph infection. I remember the excruciating pain of these boils as they grew larger, stretching the skin. Every movement was agony and sleep was out of the question. I was feverish and held my moaning to a minimum, afraid to awaken the other women. My treatment consisted of hot, wet compresses with the hope that this would hasten draining. This alone usually did not accomplish it and the physician would have to lance them. I know I would not have survived had I been in Kaiserwald or, for that matter, in Stutthof, where we were forced to pass inspection to make sure we were fit to work.

More than three years had passed and our resistance to illness, I am sure, had by this time diminished. Again, I was fortunate, I healed with only some light scarring. Occasionally we received visits from Kaiserwald's notorious commandant, Sauer, who inspected our facility to make sure we did not live too comfortably. If any contraband was found, he made sure that the offender was returned to Kaiserwald, often to be transported from there to an unknown destination. Sauer also came to see if there were some people who either were too old or ill to work and they, too, were returned to camp.

In spite of all of this, living and working in the city was profitable in other ways. A few people who had lived all their lives in Riga, and still had contact with trusted Christians, were able to receive through them some items they had hidden before going to the ghetto. These were used not only to barter for extra food, but also to bribe Walter Eggers, a soldier of low rank in the military under whose command we were placed. He was clever enough to realize that this was an opportunity to enrich himself and to accumulate a small fortune. Most of the time he looked the other way and tried to cover for us if necessary. Therefore we were able to supplement our rations from Kaiserwald with additional food.

Summer of 1944 arrived and with it the Russian army advanced. The front was only about 35 miles from Riga. The German occupation force panicked. We were apprehensive but rejoiced when we heard that we would be evacuated. How this would be accomplished no one knew. The Russians had advanced in such a way as to make an open sea route, the Baltic Sea, the only route of escape. To make us recognizable as prisoners should some of us escape, we had our hair totally shorn off; barely one millimeter of it was left on our heads. We were aghast, hardly recognizing each other, suppressing tears.

Our hope for the Russians to take over was quickly

dashed; our prayers to be liberated now that the front neared did not look like they ever would be answered. In the evening of July 29, 1944, Dr. Rudow, his sister-in-law, Zina, and Izia Pristin fled our facility. When we realized the severity of our situation, panic gripped us. The reason those three people fled was that Zina Rudow's husband, the "Aryer Rudow" (aryer, meaning Aryan), who probably had kept in touch with his wife and brother, had communicated to them that a selection was planned for the next day and advised them to lose no time and leave H.K.P. immediately.

Apparently, this escape was planned in advance. Necessary keys were on hand and the location of a safe house was already established. At the same time Boris Rudow, too, escaped from Lenta.

After the war I learned that although Boris Rudow was liberated by the Russians, he was later arrested by them. No one ever knew for sure what might have happened to him, as he was never seen again. Ultimately, Pristin and Zina Rudow married and emigrated to New York where I met with them on several occasions.

The escape of these three people left us with no doubt about the questionable chance of our own survival. We were up most of the night, fearful and guessing what might be in store for us. All through the night one could feel the unrest, hear whispering, and when dawn arrived, we discovered that several more people had fled during an air raid which had occurred during the night. I remember how angry I felt when I realized that their escape had jeopardized my own survival, but there was little time left in which to speculate if hostages would be taken for the escapees. The next day we were ordered to gather our few belongings and were told that we were going to be returned to Kaiserwald. With heavy hearts, we all climbed into the trucks that would take us back to the one place we so much dreaded. I believe, had we known what awaited us there, we might have not so docilely mounted the truck.

Eggers accompanied us on this drive, which did not take too long. We arrived at Kaiserwald at the precise moment that another Aktion, a selection, was in progress. Panic gripped us as we all were roughly pulled out of the truck, which then left immediately. We stood there and saw with terror what was happening. I still can see the nightmarish scene before my eyes: SS and overseers shouting, dust whirling in the air as many trucks, filled with screaming people, were speeding out of the camp. I had no doubt as to the destination of these vehicles. I also knew with certainty that it would be only a matter of minutes before our group would be loaded unto the next empty truck.

We stood there, huddling closely together, when out of nowhere Mr. X appeared. He instantly recognized me, seemed surprised, and after glancing over the rest of the group, motioned us to follow him. He hastily led us away from the center of all the activities to a barracks into which he pushed us, closed the door and then locked us up. We found ourselves to be in what I assumed might have been a bath house. The room was quite dark. We could not see what was happening outside, but still heard shouts and screams. Not knowing why, nor for how long we had to be waiting our turn in this place, our panic increased. Then the doors opened, and there was Mr. X, who led us out to a very quiet camp. The Aktion was over, another miracle had happened; I was saved by Mr. X. We were regrouped and were led back to the main part of the camp where the women and men were assigned to separate barracks.

The horror of having escaped certain death just a short time ago made our situation of being back in this dreadful camp more acceptable at this time. There were fewer people there and although the routine was about the same, it definitely was less strict. At night, we could hear the rumbling of cannon and "enemy" air raids as the Russian continued to encircle Riga. Through conversations with other prisoners we found out that not only in Kaiserwald, but in most other camps, Aktions had occurred. In some, anyone below 18 years and above 30 years was, without exception, liquidated. These selections were ordered as prelude to the evacuation of the Reich, as by that time the Germans knew fully that they were unable to hold off the encroaching Russia offensive.

I knew that I would be evacuated, and not knowing where made me think of escaping. There was a confused atmosphere in camp, and when I again met Mr. X a day or two later I mentioned to him that I was wondering if one could not escape by digging under the wire. He said that he believed this route would not be feasible.

Several stories of Mr. X's fate circulated: in one, that he was shipped to the front where he was shot; in another, that he had escaped Kaiserwald before the evacuation. I heard the latter story when we were on a ship that took us to Danzig. I remember wondering whether he used the idea I mentioned to him to accomplish his escape. The last I heard was that he did not survive the war. Shortly before the liberation of Stutthof, where he had been also shipped from Riga, just as we were, inmates murdered him.

I stayed at Kaiserwald for only another couple of days and then was brought back to the main HKP Wasserstrasse, the one where Inge had been. With me were another few who had been transported from our HKP to Kaiserwald and survived. I do not know how this came about, but I believe that maybe Eggers took a chance to ask for the workers who had been at HKP previously. Inge was there and we shared our experiences of the last few days. She told me that several people escaped from her place, too. We chatted and were happy to be together again. I stayed there for a few days and then we were all taken to another camp, ABA. The people who had worked there had already gone to the harbor. I do not know why they brought us there first, but then, nothing made sense anymore. We stayed only overnight, received a small food ration and were then, on August 6, 1944, brought to the harbor and loaded unto the ship, the "Bremerhafen," which was supposed to take us to Germany where we were to work.

We found ourselves, women and men, in separate sections of the ship, in the most horrible conditions; crowded and hot, several hundred people with only two toilets. I shared a narrow bunk with Inge and Vivi Misroch, another girl who also was in HKP. It was, of course, impossible to stretch out sharing the bunk with three people. Only when totally exhausted did we fall asleep on top of each other. There was no food or water, and we were all convinced that once on the high seas we would all be blown up. After four days, we landed near Danzig (Gdansk), Poland, where we disembarked. We were happy to leave this horrible ship and the nightmarish trip behind us. Just to feel solid ground under our feet made us feel more hopeful. Little did we know, at that time, that what was to follow would be more horrible than what we had experienced until now.

Not far from where we landed we saw a big grassy meadow to which we were led and allowed to stop and rest. Men and women were still separated and all of us guarded by the SS who made sure that we did not mingle. The day was blistering hot, the sun was blazing and we all were very thirsty. I have never forgotten this particular day, for the experience of having been so extremely thirsty, so parched, has always stayed with me. Sometime later, perhaps late afternoon, we were all herded toward barges which were usually used for transport of coal, cement, bricks, etc. We were rushed or pushed down into the dark hold of the barge and were so tightly squeezed in that most of us had to stand. There was no light or ventilation; the heat was unbearable. Many felt ill and I thought at times that I would suffocate. We remained this way all through the night until the morning when the barges stopped and the SS started their shouting again.

We tried as quickly as possible to climb out, otherwise beatings would rain on us again, were ordered to line up and form a column. We marched through a small town of neat, clean houses and began to hope that maybe we were lucky and things might get better for us. How were we to know that this particular road would lead us to a special kind of hell; the concentration camp Stutthof. After about six miles we arrived at the camp, and from afar it looked like a small town. There was a main street, numerous side streets and many, many barracks.

After passing through the big gate, we found ourselves on the main street and from there were led to our barracks. Each barracks was divided into two parts, A and B; each was built to hold 250 women but close to 900 were housed there. As was common, we were greeted with whips, clubs, kicks, and obscenities and we were pushed into the barracks. Several women had to share one bunk, and even then, many of us slept on the floor, tightly packed, almost on top of each other. Inge and I slept on the floor, and we were constantly stepped on. My only concern was to safeguard a little piece of bread from being stolen.

Our overseers, all convicts, were issued clubs and whips; some even had dogs. Most barracks elders were vicious and our block elder, Lenna, was no exception and did not miss an opportunity to beat us.

Next morning at 4 o'clock, we were awakened and were expected to be at roll call within three minutes. To accomplish the task of driving several hundred women out of their barracks at once, Lenna and helpers employed their whips and clubs. After roll call, which often could last several hours, we received "coffee", which was ladled into bowls shared by two women. There was hardly time to consume our bread that most of us had saved from the night before, and we cradled or slept on at night so it was not stolen. Then, we had another roll call, this time standing in the hot sun. For lunch we received approximately one quart of cabbage soup which was again shared. Most of the day was spent out in the open until evening, when we received our bread ration and a dab of margarine. After this, a repeat of the night before: a fight for a place to stretch out.

Daily, at roll call, we were "mustered" to see if we were worthy to be alive in this hell. If prisoners did not look strong enough or exhibited signs of malnutrition, had sores on their legs or rashes on their faces, they would be moved aside and to a separate barracks. We knew with a certainty what their fate would be. The chimneys belched smoke night and day! Hunger, beatings, filth, exposure to the ele-

Stutthof

ments, and whims of sadists left us in constant fear of getting selected to go "through the chimneys." These all made me fear that my struggles for staying alive, staying sane, were coming to an end. I do not know at what point we acquired our grey and blue striped prison uniform; at any rate, we now were "Zebras" too.

A transport of several thousand women arrived from Auschwitz. Among them were many from Hungary; but also from other occupied countries: Poland, Lithuania and Estonia. Through questioning, I found out where a contingency of women from Lithuania were housed, and during an idle time outside I made my way toward their barracks. The inmates of that barracks, just like us, had to spend their time outside until the next roll call. Through a fence I looked them over and could not believe my eyes when I saw the familiar face of Paula Gavronski. Paula's sister, Frieda, was married to my uncle Elias, my mothers' oldest brother.

And now, there was Paula, sitting on the dirty ground, filthy, in rags and it seemed unreal that we were meeting here. I remembered when I saw her last, in August of 1938. My mother, brother, and I were, as in most years, visiting her family in Gargzdai and Klaipeda (Memel) during our summer vacation. Paula told me that everyone in my mother's family was killed. She did not know of the fate of my aunt Hennie who resided in Kaunas (Kowno) when the Germans marched into Lithuania, and who was then sent to Estonia. When I went back the next day I could not find her and was told that she was taken to the crematorium.

There was only one thought in our minds, to try to get

out of here. When a labor detail was formed to work outside the camp, Inge and I were selected. We were transported to a farm where we were assigned to help with the harvest. I was dragging sacks of flour which must have weighed more than I. Sometimes I walked along the thresher, either feeding or unloading it, keeping pace with the machine. For us who had lived through our fourth summer of deprivation, these tasks required monumental effort. Where did I get the strength? Our day started at 3:30 a.m. and lasted until dusk.

Once when Inge fell out of the loft of the barn, most likely while stashing away hay, I was sure that she was dead when I saw her lying so still on the ground.

We were housed in a tiny room, under the roof, but did I sleep? I do not think so. I remember that in my sleep, in my dreams, I continued working and my muscles continued to be active and twitched. I am sure that the food must have been better, although I do not recall what our meals consisted of. Regardless of the hard work, we were spared eminent selection and death and for the moment kept total malnutrition at bay.

This labor assignment did not last too long, for when the harvest was complete we were returned to Stutthof. Nothing had changed. We despaired of ever leaving this gruesome place alive, as we were forced to submit again to the agonies of roll call and possible selections. We did not know what our fate eventually might be, but we did know with certainty what we could expect until then: gnawing hunger and being totally at the mercy of our criminal overseers who took great joy in beating us. We would be screamed at and addressed with obscenities such as "Jewsows", "garbage animals", "stupid cows", to mention just a few of the choice names. However, this was nothing compared with watching some of the unfortunate inmates, who were judged not strong enough, being designated for the crematorium.

We held tenaciously to one thought: to get out of this camp. Every additional day that we spent here we moved closer to the chimneys. Staying in camp during the day brought the danger of being rounded up for extermination. We heard that a big labor commando would be formed, so Inge and I made sure that we would be near the place where the registration was held. Again, we had to go through a selection before being registered. A table was set up outside the barracks and we had to file by and pass inspection. Great attention was paid to our legs to ascertain that we did not suffer from boils caused by malnutrition. There were times when I was afraid to scratch my insect bites for fear of marking my skin. Heads held high, we marched by, hoping to be chosen to leave this camp, regardless of where we might be sent. Again, the procedure of this selection was along the lines we already were used to: some to the left and some to the right, and we desperately prayed to get into the group chosen to work outside the camp.

At long last Inge and I found ourselves among a group of 1700 women selected to be transferred to another labor camp. Most women, about 1500, came from Hungary; the rest from Lithuania, Latvia, Poland and Czechoslovakia, with only about 35 women from Germany. After receiving a blanket, a metal dish, a spoon, and food ration to last for three days, we were, to our great relief, on our way out of the camp. We were guarded by 72 Lithuanian SS men and a German SS Oberscharfuehrer was our Kommandant. Our way led us first through dense forest and we, who had associated forests with extermination, were fearful that these woods might become our cemetery. We had no idea what direction we were being led or what the ultimate destination would be, so we just kept on marching.

We began to tire; most likely the guards did too, for we finally were allowed to rest and to eat some of our ration. We continued to walk for approximately 10 more miles when we reached a small railroad station where an open freight train was waiting for us. We tried to fit; all of us stood up and still there was barely enough room. Luckily, this turned out to be a short trip. When we stopped at Marienburg, we were loaded into a passenger train where most of us were able to find seats. This fact alone was a reason to start reassessing our situation and to begin to hope again.

We travelled throughout the night and arrived in the early morning in Argenau. An approximately two-hour march brought us to a clearing at the edge of a forest where we saw what looked like a small tent city. There were many tents. We called them "Finnenzelte", Finnish tents, which were round and constructed out of plywood. They originally were designed to house 12 horses, but 60 women were assigned to each tent. There was a kitchen with open air and with several large kettles of about 70 gallons capacity. We found potatoes, and hurriedly concocted a soup of unpeeled, diced potatoes.

Meanwhile, we found a supply of straw which was brought to our tents and after we ate, we went to sleep. It was late summer and the weather was still mild, so that living in the tents did not present any hardship for us. In the morning, labor details were put together, spades handed out and most of the women, guarded by the Lithuanian SS, went to work digging ditches for defense purposes.

Our commandant, Heinrich Binding from Berlin, who apparently had never been in charge of this kind of "enterprise" before, was fairly decent. In contrast, the Lithuanians treated us brutally and would gladly have shot us if the commandant would have allowed it. Some of us stayed in camp for we were needed to help run it. I was chosen to work in the kitchen detail and stayed up many hours at night tending the kettles. After almost everyone left the camp and I completed my tasks in the kitchen I was allowed to catch up on my sleep. I would get my blanket, walk to the edge of the forest and there among tall weeds I would lie, warmed by the mild, late autumn sun. Most of the guards were away; it was very quiet. I was not seen by anyone and I kept thinking that this surely must be heaven.

To this very day, when on camping trips I see a similar area, I recall the bliss I felt then.

One morning, when I was watching the kettles, Binding passed by as was his habit, and stopped to talk to me. After a few minutes of talking about some things concerning the camp, he switched to a more personal subject. He told me how he missed his family, how lonesome he was, that there were very few people to talk to and then asked me if I would consider being his Konkubine. I was so shocked that, not thinking clearly, I blurted out the first thing which came to my mind: that I was married and that I just could not think of it. In back of my mind, also, was the thought of how I possibly could tolerate to be the kept women of not only a German, but also of my jailer. But I did not tell him that.

I was lucky that he took my refusal quite good naturedly and within a very short time he had established a relationship with another young Jewish girl. I must say, that he treated her well; he took excellent care of her when she later became seriously ill.

Many years later I thought of this incident and realized how naive I must have been. Given the same circumstances, would I have given the same answer today?

Then Inge came down with scarlet fever and had to go to the Lazarett, the tent reserved for ill prisoners. When Binding mentioned that he might have to send Inge back to Stutthof and I told him that I would accompany her, he questioned me if I was aware of what would happen to me if I did. I knew of the consequences but really did not care, for life at this time did not mean anything to me without my friend. I told him so and he decided to put off this decision for a few more days.

A few years ago, when visiting a woman named Margie Strauss who was with us in the same camp, I was introduced to her husband as "the girl who saved her life." I could not recall any instance when I could have performed such a heroic act.

She explained that she, too, had scarlet fever and laid

next to Inge in the Lazarette. She pointed out that when I was able to "organize" some hot potato water from the kitchen, I used to bring it to Inge and then she always shared it with Putti, as Margie was then called. She attributed her recovery to the healing properties of this hot potion.

After about a month, the work was complete and we had to leave this camp site. It seemed liked we walked almost all day before we finally arrived at a work camp known as a Schluessel Muehle, a mill which had served and was still, to a lesser extent, serving as a prison camp for Russians. The camp was divided by barbed wire. The Russians were guarded by the army; we by the SS. We wished that we, too, could have had the Wehrmacht as guards. An army camp was situated not too far from us where soldiers from the front came to rest before going back again. Some passed by occasionally and were horrified when they saw how we were treated. They professed that they had no knowledge of what was happening in the concentration camps and that they were kept in total ignorance of our situation. They treated us decently and after seeing our plight managed to bring some bread.

One soldier gave me a fine-tooth comb, made out of wood. This comb was a very coveted item, virtually a treasure, for it could assist in disposing of lice, should there be any on the scalp. He gave me his name and asked me to remember him kindly in case the war would be lost.

Soon we had to leave, and we made our way, marching for approximately ten hours, to camp Korben. Korben was located near the Polish town of Thorn, or what is now called Torun. Again, we found numerous round plywood tents that would house 60 women. There were two pumps. Most of time, only one was in good enough working condition to deliver water to the entire camp of 1700 prisoners, the kitchens, and the private apartments of the Kommandant. There were neither washing or toilet facilities to be found, and the pressing need of both demanded that we find a fast solution to these problems. If a woman with keen eyesight and a fast hand was lucky enough to have gotten hold of an empty marmalade pail, it would become the possession of her entire tent. In the evening the entire tent turned into a washroom. Any woman who was still clinging to some remnant of her former life, to some customs, some habits ingrained from childhood, would wash herself from head to toe in cold water. We took turns waiting for each other so we could use the pail.

The Death March

L ater in November, when we received a little stove for our tents, we would stand around it naked, drying off in its warmth, for towels were rarely obtainable. We used part of our meager margarine ration, a mere speck to begin with, as a beauty cream for our faces and to smooth sore and rough skin. This was more important to us than to smear it on our bread. Was this vanity? Looking back, I do not believe that it was. I think that we tried at all costs to preserve a shred of our dignity, of our self-image. This small action alone proved that we were not ready to give up.

We all were concerned about keeping discipline regarding hygiene, for we hoped to prevent outbreaks of infectious diseases which struck and liquidated similar camps. Now we had to deal with the insurmountable problem of the latrines, as there were none when we arrived. Immediately a work detail was formed to excavate deep trenches about 500-600 feet from the tents. Women walked to the edge and then used these excavations as toilets. When winter approached, this process became an ordeal; we then were exposed to rain and snow.

I came up with an idea which everyone, including our Kommandant, agreed with. I "designed" and was put in charge of digging an underground latrine. At a new site, we excavated a deeper and bigger area, and formed a ramp to go down to a platform along which we dug a trench. We got some tree stumps and laid them across the trench to be used as seats. We took pine branches and covered the entire excavation, so when using the latrine we were somewhat sheltered from the elements. This project was a success, but a short lived one. After a succession of heavy rainstorms, the entire excavation collapsed. If it had been colder, as was the case later on, I am sure everything would have frozen solid and the cave-in might have been prevented. As winter progressed, many of us suffered from dysentery and from either bladder or kidney infections. Many were not able to reach the latrines in time and we always had a busy latrine cleaning work force.

A commission from Stutthof came to inspect the camp, to see if our work force was still intact. Fortunately, we always passed inspection. On those days they would rarely find any ill women in the tents. Almost every woman, regardless of how sick or even when close to death, would leave the camp to go to work.

We had no light and again we came up with a solution. We made our own little oil lamp. We hollowed out a raw potato and made a wick by pulling some threads from rags or a blanket. Then we filled the potato with margarine which we took turns donating and dipped the wick in it. As the winter progressed with more rain, snow and cold, our tents became saturated with water which seeped through the cracks in the plywood. We dug a two to three-foot trench around our tent, piled the dirt vertically against the outside of the tent, covered the roof with moss, and then tried to cover the rest of the tent with evergreen branches. This was a definite improvement, for we managed to insulate ourselves somewhat from the cold and dampness.

The cold became bitter and we had no adequate clothes. Only after about 40 women had died did Stutthof ship some winter clothes. We each received, among other items, striped prison underwear and a coat. Starvation, dysentery, and hard work coupled with extreme cold limited our chances of survival. The mortality rate increased; almost every day four or five women died. Others became what we called a "Muselman." One would pass these poor human beings and see that they were marked by death. Their eyes were dead; they shuffled instead of walking; the skin often looked edematous and transparent; they hardly ever talked; they had given up and it seemed that they already had died inside; physical death followed soon.

Most of the German speaking women were chosen to help run the camp, so Inge and I, among others, became Kapos. Our functions were unlike the ones in Auschwitz and other camps for we acted as liaison between the SS and the other inmates who did not speak German. We tried under difficult circumstances to do the best for the inmates and to contribute to the smooth running of the camp. We did our utmost to bridge the language barrier of the Hungarian women and we quickly learned a few Hungarian phrases to convey what was expected of them or to notify them of new developments. In general, the Hungarian women had a very difficult time accepting their almost hopeless situation and they presented many problems. We tried to help but were often powerless to do so.

These women had been transferred to Stutthof from Auschwitz, where in the summer of 1944, they were taken, suddenly, without warning, out of their homes and transported to a special kind of hell. Many became mentally disturbed and lost their will to live. They could not adhere to the discipline of keeping themselves clean and did not want to wash themselves. Due to poor hygiene, they harbored great amounts of lice and it was suggested that they should sleep in the nude, wrapped in their blankets, and expose their clothes to frosty air during the night. Not only did they come from a warmer climate but, in contrast to us who were already living through our fourth winter, this was their first one and most were unable to follow this suggestion because they were too cold.

Inge and I worked inside the camp wherever we were needed. If a commission from Stutthof was expected to control our camp, we prepared the women for the expected visit. We conveyed to them the importance of their cooperation so that we could be sure that our camp would pass inspection. We also worked on the burial detail--deaths occurred more frequently as the winter progressed. We carried the dead, without their clothes, to the edge of the forest and defied the order of digging the grave several feet deep. The ground was frozen solidly, we were cold and weak and managed to dig just deep enough to barely accommodate the bodies. We really did not worry about the consequences when the ground would thaw in spring; we knew that we would not be here to witness it. Once, when we carried a dead Hungarian woman, we thought she sighed. We were terribly frightened, thinking that she was still alive. Hanka, a Czechoslovakian who had studied medicine for several semesters, explained that dead people sometimes emit a small amount of air.

There was no shortness of firewood living in the forest. Many times I felled trees. When did I ever learn to do that? Not only that, but it was short of a miracle that I did not get killed in the process. Two of us sawed a tree and when it started to sway we quickly stepped back when it fell. The wood was used to cook our food in the six 70 gallon kettles, and for our little stoves in the tents.

Sometimes I also worked in the kitchen. At night during a "kettle watch" I would sit, wrapped in a blanket, on top of a warm kettle that was filled with coffee for the early morning after we had finished with roll call. The kitchen was situated in the open with the kettles stationed side by side. A flat roof rested on supports, and we wove birch branches around the back and sides to form a windbreaker; the front was left open. I remember one day working in the kitchen when the kettles were full and we were cooking soup. I kept the fire supplied with wood and was stirring the soup when suddenly the fire became too hot and the soup started to boil over. I frantically tried to lower the heat and the only way I could think of was to pick up a pail of water and dowse the fire. I did not think of the consequences; the resulting steam hit my legs and burned me.

The winter continued and so did our hardship; hunger, cold and disease claimed more victims. Many more women died, emaciated, dehydrated and weakened from bouts of dysentery. I always feared that I too might fall victim to this often fatal camp disease, but hoped that I would be immune. Then one day I experienced the dreaded symptoms. Of course, there were no remedies to be obtained aside from what was rumored to somewhat alleviate the suffering. I applied a well-known, home remedy of heat, and was able to warm a rock under the kettle. I clutched the rock to my abdomen whenever my cramps became severe. I also scraped off small amounts of charcoal, which I ate, hoping that it would stop the diarrhea. Fortunately, I had a mild case and it abated before my body was weakened too much by it.

Our saving grace was that the commandant was decent; if it were not for him, our Lithuanian guards, under the command of their SS commandant would have completed their own version of the "Final Solution". As it was, they gave full reign to their sadistic streaks by brutally hitting our women with the butts of their guns, regardless whether outside on work detail or inside the camp.

The year 1945 began. What would this year bring us? Was there any chance of us surviving at all? We had lived for so long completely isolated that we did not know how the war had progressed up to now. We knew that something bothered our German camp administrators; they seemed to convey some uneasiness, some nervousness. Then at night we heard some distant rumbling and suspected that the Russian front was advancing. We were elated; the hour of liberation was nearing. Would we be alive to experience this so desperately prayed for event?

Shortly, at evening roll call, we were ordered to vacate the camp the following day and to start our march farther into the Reich. Very early the next morning, at roll call, food supplies were handed out for the trip. We already had fashioned some sort of bags from paper sacks or rags which were to hold our food ration for the march.

We received instructions; among them one that sounded ominous: "The SD (security service) will transport by truck women who are unable to walk and the ones in the tents for the seriously ill." Ten guards would be stationed with these women and we knew what that meant; we knew how bloodthirsty these Lithuanians were. We implored everyone to say that they were able to walk and warned them that their lives would be in danger should they stay behind. This way we were able to change the minds of a few women who had, at the beginning, decided to be transported by truck.

When we were finished forming our column, just before leaving the camp, I saw a young girl in the group that was to stay behind. She definitely looked as if she was able to walk and stayed close to a woman who, I surmised, was her mother. There was no doubt in my mind, having seen this tragedy played out before, that she wanted to stay with her mother regardless of the consequences. I begged her to come with us, but she did not budge. I did not know if she understood me; time was running out. We were prodded to leave. In desperation I hit her with my hand, pulled her out of the huddle of sick women with all my strength, and forced her into our already moving column. Still, we had to leave 183 women behind in camp.

We started our march, our last fight for survival. A few minutes after the last of the women left, we heard the rattle of machine guns from the direction of the camp. What we feared had come to pass! There were only corpses for the SD to transport. A few days later, toward the end of our march, I found the girl who I had separated from her mother and begged her to forgive me for having her treated so roughly. She cried and told me that she understood my motives.

We were aware of secret orders that, should the front advance, no inmates were to be taken alive by the enemy. We had no illusions as to what lay before us and knew that whatever it was would require a strength that none of us still possessed.

We were herded through snow and ice by our tormentors, the sixty-two Lithuanian SS. We walked through woods which were densely covered with snow taxing our strength even more. The open roads could not always be used by us, as they were often jammed by German civilians fleeing in carriages drawn by horses. As time passed, it became more difficult to keep up and when the first women stumbled, it took only seconds before we heard shots and we all realized what could be in store for us; anyone who could not keep up and lagged behind would meet the same fate. Every woman made a heroic effort to keep up. They assisted and encouraged each other, but for some whose spirits did not break but whose bodies did, it was the end of their tormented voyage. Our murderous guards were always ready to satisfy their sadistic yearning for blood and if some faltered or stumbled the guards would quickly pull them out and shoot them.

We were on the road four days and covered an estimated 96 km (60 mi). During the night in which we walked, terrorized, in what seemed a nightmare, eighty-seven women were murdered by the Lithuanians. A long column of bedraggled, exhausted, weak, and hungry women continued their march through snow and cold. Only the fear of being shot if we stopped and the thought that we might be near our goal, near our freedom, pushed us on and prevented us from dropping out. But something else encouraged us. In ditches by the road we would occasionally see discarded German uniforms and would smile at each other knowingly. But our guards had other thoughts. They told us, smiling sadistically, that we should not rejoice as yet; none of us would be alive when the Russians arrived. There was no doubt in our minds as to their intentions. We searched for an opportunity to escape from our vicious guards but none that would not have meant almost instant death presented itself. Our guards surrounded us and never let us out of their sight.

On rare occasions we were allowed a short rest stop. Not having water to drink we used snow to refresh ourselves.

At night, totally exhausted, we would stumble into dark stables. I remember one time when we finally were allowed to stop for the night and entered a stable. I could not see anything and was completely disoriented as to where I was stepping. I groped for a space to fit my tired body. I was so exhausted that I just did not care where the space was located. During the night, having spent these few hours in almost a stupor-like sleep, I heard some stomping, animal sounds and, at times, clanking of metal. In the morning I found that I had slept so close to a cow that I was surprised that I was not kicked by the animal.

Toward the end of the fourth day, the almost totally drunk Lithuanians decided to escape the fast advancing enemy. Later on, I heard that they wanted to shoot us all before fleeing. Our German commandant was arguing with the Lithuanian commandant of the guard and absolutely forbade him, under the threat of shooting him, to harm us, so they all left. After having passed Bromberg (Bidgodz), a few miles outside town, we again stopped for the night at a farm. During the night, Inge and I whispered to each other about what we should do; should we wait and see what might happen? I suggested that we try to leave, that we might never get another chance. During these last few years we had made few decisions ourselves and it was easy to continue to let things just happen to us. We decided then that we would try to escape, and towards dawn we both quietly stepped around sleeping bodies and tiptoed to the outside. We thought we had been unobserved, but shots rang out. Inge sustained a small wound when the bullet whizzed by. This all seems like a dream were it not for the scar on her head.

We quickly crossed the main road and ducked between houses. We walked through the snowy countryside away from the main road which we already knew was jammed with civilians and retreating military. We were lucky that this area was isolated for we were still dressed in our striped prison garb and we did not want to meet anyone who might have gotten suspicious. We passed a very small, modest house which looked deserted. After we were certain that it was unoccupied, we entered it. The Germans who lived there had quickly abandoned it when the front advanced, for we found food still on the table. We inspected a few small rooms and then came to what appeared to be the living room. I will never forget the moment when I saw on the wall a large, framed picture of Hitler. What did I feel at this time and what were my thoughts? Savage rage surfaced that choked me. Like a wild woman, I proceeded to tear up his picture with a vengeance - I tore the eyes out first. I would soon be 23 and after years of untold, intense suffering this would be my first and only act of celebration.

After a couple of days, two young men knocked on the door and we became alarmed. It turned out that they were Polish civilians who had escaped from forced labor and were looking for shelter. We shared the house and whatever food there was. A stable near the house sheltered some animals and the young men slaughtered a pig and milked a cow. We all were free, we had a roof over our heads, we ate our fill and felt that this was heaven on earth! We still were not able to eat large amount of foods and felt ill if we did so. The sounds of the battle continued, and the little house shook as the front drew nearer.

On January 5, 1945, a Russian soldier on an almost white horse approached the house, and he told us that the Germans had left and they were now occupying this area. I felt as if the Messiah had come on his white horse and liberated us. Our dreams, wishes and hopes were fulfilled; we were liberated --and alive!

I understand that after Inge and I walked off the farm, several more did too. However, many women remained on the farm even after the commandants had themselves fled. There was a rumor that the older of the two, Wilhelm Anton, shot himself.

Freedom for the women did not last long. According to Feige Szander (Brodie), with whom I visited in San Francisco in 1987, the owner of the farm notified the SD, the security police. Within a short time, new guards materialized. The following morning the women were forced to walk again, and toward evening they arrived at a prison, where they were fed. She also told me that the prison was almost totally empty except for two Jewish prisoners from Warsaw. They told the new arrivals that the SS had plans to take the women to a forest near Konitz on the following morning and shoot them. But fate intervened. In the morning, after heavy fighting, a Russian on a very light-colored horse arrived at the prison gate. He was a general and asked the women who they were. When they explained that they had been concentration camp inmates, he did not believe them and shouted that there were no more Jews alive and that they should tell him the truth. Only after Feige and a woman from Riga spoke to him in Russian and Yiddish did disbelief change to joy and he excitedly shouted to his companion, who had followed him on horseback, that there were still Jews alive. It turned out that the general was Jewish himself. I wonder whether the two Russians on horses who told us that we were free, were the same.

Inge and I remained at the house for a little while longer and then retraced our steps to Bydgozc. Somewhere along the way we were held up by advancing Russians who thought us to be spies. I guess they thought that our prison uniform was not genuine. I attempted to converse in Russian, in which I was not fluent, but sufficient to convince them that we were who we claimed to be and we were able to get out of our predicament. I was fortunate in that a major who was Jewish overheard me and made sure that we were not harassed anymore.

Liberation

Once in Bidgozc we tried to find a place to stay and were assigned to a large apartment occupied by Russian military. In exchange for cleaning and cooking, we received room and board. We had our own room and the men were decent. They were somewhat fearful and in the habit of always locking their rooms. One night, when Inge went to the bathroom, one of the men mistook her for a spy and went after her with his gun. I practiced my Russian on him and apparently succeeded in calming him down. My limited knowledge of Russian language assisted me several times in the months to follow. Having heard my mother speak this language at times and having spent the years from 1939 through the camp years among people who spoke Russian enabled me to communicate in it.

We cleaned the apartment, cooked and served the meals and afterwards cleaned the table and washed the dishes. I always poured the leftover vodka from the glasses into an empty bottle. I cannot recall why I ever wanted to do such a thing as I was not in the habit of drinking. It is possible that after years of deprivation I was loathed to throw anything away. What I remember was that I had a bottle of this saved up vodka with me when traveling through Poland in an unheated transport train. I am sure that my feet would have frozen if not for the few sips I took from my bottle. I felt the alcohol go straight to my feet and ignite. What a pleasant feeling that was, when the heat coursed through my frozen body.

When we decided to leave Bidgozc, we boarded a train and, not really knowing where we wanted to go, acted like homing pigeons; we came from Riga, so we headed back east. All of a sudden, I realized that Riga was occupied by the Russians and, having lived there under Russian occupation from 1940 until 1941, I knew exactly what to expect. I remember that it felt as if someone was telling me to quickly change directions and called out to Inge that we should not go back to Riga. When the train slowed, we both jumped out. We had heard that Lodz, one of the largest towns in Poland, had a Jewish Community Center which was assisting former Jewish prisoners to find housing and to facilitate the search for families who were separated during deportation.

We arrived in Lodz and found that many other liberated prisoners were there too. We found a house in which two or three Jewish men lived. They, too, were liberated and were without families. They agreed that we could stay with them if we would take care of the household and do the cooking while they went to work. There were not enough rooms and I slept on a sofa in the living room. Everything worked out and we settled into a routine until the night one of the men pounced on me. I really had to struggle with him and made enough noise to bring everybody running. We decided not to stay there any longer and set out to find other lodgings. We then were able to secure a small room somewhere else. Inge did not know where her parents were and decided to look for them and we separated. Soon afterwards, I met a girl who mentioned that she was staying with a group that occupied a large apartment and that there was room for me, too, if I wanted to live with them. I was very happy to accept her offer for I did not like to be by myself, missing companionship since Inge had left.

The group I joined was made up of former concentration camp inmates from many countries. We were all used to group living and got along well. All of us were waiting for only one thing, the end of the war. Until then we lived in a state of suspended animation. What was uppermost in everyone's mind was the uncertainty of knowing what had happened to family members. We listened to the news constantly and fervently hoped that the Russian army would continue to advance. Then came the long-awaited news! I remember the day when, as usual, several people crowded around the radio and as there were not enough chairs, I sat on a little footstool right in front of the radio when we heard that the Germans had surrendered! This was May 8, 1945.

I could now plan for the future; I had to find a way to go to the United States. After some thinking, I decided that I needed to first find the U.S. forces. I set out to follow the advancing Red Army with the goal of reaching Berlin, approximately 350 miles from Lodz. I hitchhiked, riding on trucks and trains. Often, the trucks were part of convoys following the troops and I felt that there was safety in numbers. My Russian really helped me, and I was able to make myself understood. As not every convoy was going toward my destination, I had to get off at times and look for some other transportation.

The last stretch of the trip I covered by train which mostly carried Army personnel. During the trip I had gotten acquainted with a small group of Russian officers who made some room for me to sit in their compartment. Toward evening, the train stopped at Grunewald, a once wealthy suburb of Berlin, and everybody had to get off. The officers told me that I could follow them and when they took over a house that belonged to a German family, I was permitted to stay with them. It was fairly late by the time we finished eating and then all of them went upstairs to sleep. I stayed downstairs and, fully dressed, laid down on a sofa, grateful to have found a place to stretch out and rest for a few hours.

I was almost asleep when I realized that I was not alone and recognized one of the officers who, feeling amorous, decided to pay me a visit. Luck was on my side. There was some light coming from the adjoining room and I was able to see. All I can remember was that I ran into the next room, which apparently was the dining room, and stopped behind a table. When he came after me I was able to evade him by going around the table. I felt panicky and thought that this just could not be happening to me, not after all these years! I had to get away! I ran toward the porch through which we had entered a few hours ago. The Russian was close enough to get hold of me momentarily. I tore open the door and ran out into the black night, but he still got hold of my arm. Fear and anger must have given me strength to shake him loose and continue to run away from him. Because it was so dark, he was unable see me and I quickly crouched behind some bushes to hide until I was sure that he had given up finding me.

I then assessed the situation I was in and it was far from pleasant. Here I was, in the middle of the night, not a soul on the street and none of the houses around had lights on to guide me. Still shocked and scared, I started to move away when I thought that I heard some footsteps. I panicked and ran across the street and knocked at the first house I came to, begging to be let in quickly. When someone hesitantly opened the door just a tiny bit, I explained what had happened to me and asked if I could stay the night. They agreed immediately and let me stay on the porch and made up a bed for me on a chaise. I thought how ironic this whole situation was. Here were Germans hiding me from the Russians, my liberators!

The following morning, I asked if I could stay another couple of hours before leaving, just to make sure that I would not run into any of the officers. My hosts were agreeable, and a few hours later I was on my way. I had been informed that there were no Americans anywhere near or in Berlin, but most likely could be found in Wittenberg by the Elbe River. Again, I hitched a ride on a Russian truck and found myself going through Berlin. I passed our apartment which was one of the few houses still standing. Seeing the house in which I had spent my entire life until I fled Berlin on January 30, 1939, I felt as if I had been having a bad dream, as if nothing was real anymore. A little more than six years had passed from that day in 1939, and it seemed as if had lived through a lifetime of nightmares. This was May 16, 1945. Only eight days after Germany had surrendered. Wherever I looked there were either burned out houses or ruins, many still smoldering.

Later on, I again had to get off the truck as it was not going where I was headed. I was lucky that another truck gave me a lift close to Wittenberg, from where I walked the rest of the way into the city. The only problem with this driver was that occasionally he tried to drive with one hand and that his free hand started to wander toward my knees. I avoided an open confrontation, as I did not want to anger him. I was worn out; I needed this ride desperately to reach the end of this difficult journey. Going around the next curve, I inched away from him, and at the end it did not present much of a problem; the road had become narrower and winding and the driver had to use both hands to keep the truck on the road.

Once in Wittenberg, I thought I would find the U.S. forces but failed to see any. In fact, I still saw some Russian soldiers. I questioned some people and was told that they were stationed across the river. I walked toward the river and when I came near the bank, I found a grassy incline with many people sitting there. I was very tired and sat down to rest among the other displaced persons. I never had a chance to ask anyone what they all were waiting for when I turned around and saw my first U.S. soldiers. There were two of them on a raft made of tree trunks and they were just about to push off and cross the river. I ran to the edge and called out that I wanted to go to America and hands stretched out to help me jump across several feet of water. Another few seconds and I would not have made it. Later on, I found out that some of the people there had crossed the river in the other direction in order to go east- back home- for many had worked for the Germans and were forced to leave their countries.

I was taken to a headquarters of the U.S. occupation forces and immediately got something to eat- my first American food. I told them what had happened to me over the last few years and one of the soldiers offered to write a letter to my parents to tell them that I was alive. I had to search my memory for their address, the only thing I was sure of was the name of the town, Mount Vernon, New York. I could not remember what the number of the house was or the name of the street. The soldier did some juggling and came up with something which looked like an address to which mail could be delivered.

The next day I was driven to a place which apparently was used as a collection center for displaced persons. After waiting for a couple of hours, we were taken to a railroad station and we boarded a train. It is amazing that I never questioned the fact where I was being sent. I probably had the good sense to realize that it would be best for me to have someone else make the decisions and was confident

that those decisions would be in my best interest. I felt relieved that I could just coast along, that I could stop fighting
for my life, that the worst was over. Little did I know that
this interlude only lasted a short time and that I would soon
have to start plotting and scheming again.

The train brought us to Salzwedel, a displaced persons
camp. This place was huge. Ironically, Salzwedel used to be
a training camp for the German Army. We were well taken
care of there. We had good food and the rooms were comfortable. There was nothing to do but eat, sleep and take
walks on the immense grounds. There were people from
many European nations to talk to and everyone had a story
to tell.

Not long after I arrived at Salzwedel, I experienced pain
in my abdomen which I attributed to the food. After a few
days it became apparent that the food was not to be blamed;
the pain became more localized and I was so uncomfortable
that I asked to see a doctor. I was told where to find him and
walked across the compound to the administration buildings. Once there, I saw a long line of DP's waiting to be seen
by a physician. At first, the doctor was not able to diagnose
my complaint, but after I told him that I had not had my
periods for over three years, he concluded that my problem was gynecological and that I would most likely begin
my cycle soon. He was amazed when I told him that, as far
as I knew, all or most of the women inmates had not men-
struated in years. We had first attributed this phenomenon
to something the Germans had put into our food, but then
came to the conclusion that starvation and constant terror

were attributing factors. In fact, we were grateful for this omission in our already miserable lives.

After a few days, the process of registering us began. I had no papers to prove who I was, what my name was, where I was born, or where I came from. I had only one thought in my mind: to get to the U.S. That meant to a port in order to embark on a boat to the States. With this in mind, I picked Le Havre. I think the reason I picked a French harbor instead of one in Holland, which might have been closer, was that I spoke a passable French. So, when my turn came and I was asked what nationality I was, I answered without hesitation in my best German- accented-French that I was from France and became immediately a French DP. Of course, they believed me; I could have told them anything but that I was American or English.

My plan worked and I found myself on a train bound for Paris. Still, my grandiose plan was almost foiled. During the next couple of hours, I observed that one girl in particular was watching me closely. I wondered why. She then came to me and said that she knew that I was not French and accused me of being a German spy. After I told her about what had happened to me during the last few years and what my plans for the future were, she realized that she had made a mistake. For a little while, she really had me scared. I just could not have tolerated another delay. By the end of the trip we became very friendly, and she offered to take me to her aunt's apartment, which was located in Bobigny, a Paris suburb near the Bourget Airport. After we arrived in Paris, we took the Metro and then a bus and arrived at her aunt's place and where I was made welcome. Denise's uncle was still a POW and I promised that I would only stay with them until he returned and claimed the bed that I was sleeping in. The apartment was quite small, but I was happy to be there. This was May 29, 1945. It had taken me three weeks to get from Lodz to Paris.

Not only was I without any money, but I realized that I would have to start to adjust to civilization, for the laws that had governed me the last few years were not in effect anymore. The idea that I could just get on a boat and sail to America was at best a dream that had sustained me through many difficult hours. I had to start someplace and decided to contact a Jewish agency in Paris, which assisted me with some money and advised me to get in touch with the U.S Consulate. I then decided to go to the American Red Cross to ask them if they would help me to get in touch with my parents. I located them in a big, posh building in the Place Vendome. I told them of my problem and that I was not certain of my parents' complete address. I got a very definite negative response; they stated emphatically that their only purpose was to assist the armed forces. I have never forgiven them for this and to this day the Red Cross has never received a donation from me.

I was so disappointed that I started to cry as I walked down the hall to the exit. Suddenly, someone spoke to me and asked me if he could help me. When I turned around, I saw an American soldier. Judging by my accent, he said, he thought that I was from Germany. It turned out that he, a German refugee living now with his family in the U.S.A., had observed me talking to the Red Cross representative. His name was Helmut Hertz and he told me that his wife and children lived in Rochester, N.Y. He then offered to write to his mother who lived in New York City to ask her if she would help to locate my parents.

The only facts that I was positively sure of was their name and that they lived in Mount Vernon, N.Y. This great lady quickly got hold of a Westchester telephone book, and in no time found the name and address. This was fairly easily accomplished for there were, besides my parents and brother, no other people in the U.S. with the name of Arpadi.

Two or three years earlier, Inge had the opportunity to have someone mail a letter to her aunt in Berlin, who was married to a German and had been able to continue living there during the war. Inge had asked her aunt to write to my parents to let them know that I had so far survived. At that time, I still could recall their address. This was the only time that my parents had indirectly heard of me, but so many years had passed since that day until May 1945, when a letter with an APO return address arrived and was put on the staircase leading to their apartment.

My mother told me that she saw the letter, did not think that it was important, so did not go down to pick it up, knowing that my father would be home soon and then bring the mail up. When he came up, he had the letter in his hand, puzzled about who from the army would send them a letter. My mother, still unsuspecting, continued with whatever she was doing when she heard my father shouting that

I was alive and that this letter was written by a soldier in Germany. They immediately wrote to the soldier who had sent the note, asking him for more details, but he replied that I just had passed through and that he did not know my whereabouts.

Mrs. Hertz got in touch with my parents and because they must have been incoherent at the news, she made a list of what to send me. I soon received not only money but also a package with clothes, some toilet articles and, of all things, even lipstick. I still can remember how a mere lipstick could have brought me such joy! I had continued wearing a skirt which I had fashioned by hand from an old camp blanket and it felt luxurious to finally shed this rag and put on some decent clothes. I felt that I had taken another step toward normalizing my life and adjusting to civilization.

Denise's uncle wrote that he was coming back, and I had to look for another place to stay. I wanted to continue living in Bobigny, for I liked the quiet, small village atmosphere. Denise had become my good friend and I felt that I was not completely alone; at least there was someone I could talk to. I also could reach Paris by either walking or taking a bus to Porte de La Vilette and from there, the Metro to Paris. I started to look at rooms, searching for one which would fit my budget. One day I passed by a bistro which advertised that they had a room to rent. The price I was quoted was most reasonable and I agreed to rent it. The room was located in back of the building where one could enter the rooms from a narrow walkway. The layout was not unlike modern motel rooms of today, with one exception; there was no space one could park a car. Instead, a wire fence separated a narrow path which led to the back yards of small residential houses.

I paid my month's rent, gathered my few belongings and moved in. I went to Paris a few times to visit the U.S. Embassy to start proceedings to obtain my American visa and began to get acquainted with the city. I loved exploring Paris and delayed getting back to Bobigny in the evening, for when I returned to my place, I felt quite lonely as there was not much to do or anyone to talk to. Denise had started a job and I did not see her often and felt sort of isolated. On nice days, I would take some walks and sometimes take a chair out of my room and sit in in the sun, reading.

Paris, 1945

A month passed and my landlord came by and asked for the next month's rent which I gave him. Still, he did not seem to be satisfied. He was agitated and, speaking quite rapidly, indicated that I still owed him some money. I was at a loss to understand why he continued to insist that the payment I made was insufficient. After asking him several times to give me the reason for his demand, he did not come up with an answer. I then told him firmly in my most concise French that I already had paid him the agreed amount and that I refused to pay him an additional sum. Furiously, he left my room and I felt proud to have weathered another crisis.

A short time later, there was another knock on my door and a policeman was there requesting me to present my identification papers and registration. Needless to say, I did not possess any official documents except a little slip of paper, sort of a temporary identity card. This apparently was not sufficient, and he kept insisting that I show him my registration card. "A registration? To what?" I kept asking over and over again; I absolutely could not understand what kind of registration he was referring to and told him that I could not produce any other papers. I could see that he became more frustrated and impatient by the minute and finally announced that he was going to take me to the police precinct.

Once there we went through the same scene without results, until someone hit on a bright idea. They got hold of Jewish policemen who, with the aid of some Yiddish complementing his French, explained the facts of life to me: I was living in a brothel. My landlord wanted his cut and the police wanted my "work" registration. No wonder that my room was so inexpensive, and my landlord was so positive that I was withholding what he thought was rightfully to be his extra income.

I was informed that I now could leave, but I was requested to present myself once a month at this precinct. I guess they may not have quite believed me and I was sort of on "parole." There was one more stipulation: I was to submit to a Wassermann test, a blood test for syphilis.

After I returned to my room, a middle-aged couple came to my door and introduced themselves. They told me that they lived across the walkway and that they had been watching me and that they could not understand why I, an obviously nice girl, would live in a place of this sort. After I told them how I came about to rent the room in this particular location, they immediately asked me to stay with them. I lived with them for several months and they treated me with great affection as if I was one of their own family, which consisted of two teenage boys still living at home and a daughter who was married and not living too far from them.

Only one incident almost threatened my peaceful days. I was called to the Health Department and told that my Wasserman test was positive. I could not believe this, protested vigorously and demanded to be retested. The Health Department also may have had some doubt, and they permitted me to be tested at the American Hospital in Neuilly. This time the test came back negative.

My parents continued to send me packages containing items which were scarce in France and very hard to obtain for the country was still reeling from the effects of the German occupation. Of course, the packages were joyfully shared by all of us.

I felt that I needed to do something more useful than I was doing to fill my days until I received my visa to the States, but in Bobigny, there were no opportunities for me to do so. I now was able to give some thought to the future and it occurred to me that although I knew how to do many things, I really did not have a profession which would enable me to obtain a job once I arrived in America. One year in a prestigious fashion designing school in Berlin, taking courses in hand sewn glove making and millinery, did not seem to be adequate to enter the job market.

One day when I was in Paris, I passed a Beauty School and decided to stop in to inquire about their curriculum. The course would teach three different subjects: anatomy, facials and make-up and body massage, which at time was called Swedish massage. At the end of this course I would be required to take a test, and upon completion would receive a diploma. This school was accredited and I was assured that after I graduated I would not encounter any difficulties obtaining a job either in Paris or, for that matter anywhere else. The tuition quoted was so high that I could not see how I could possibly afford to sign up. I explained my previous and present circumstances and that I could not ask my parents for any additional assistance, as they themselves were recent emigrants. I also told them that I was going to look for a job and then might be able to take their classes. I guess my luck held for they offered me a job to clean the beauty parlor that they owned, which was situated downstairs in the same building as the school, and in lieu of payment I would be allowed to take their classes.

Of course, I accepted this offer, and immediately set out to find a room in Paris. The school was located close to the Rue de Rivoli, and I found a room in a small hotel on Rue St. Honore near Les Halles. This was an ideal location, not too far from the school and in walking distance of many interesting and important places. The room was long and narrow and looked out over a very busy street. Very early in the morning, at dawn, a noise started made any more sleep impossible.

Les Halles was the central food market for all of Paris. Merchants brought their merchandise and buyers for stores and restaurants selected and bought. In fact, Jacques Lefebre, my host from Bobigny, worked there loading meat and sometimes I walked over to say hello to him.

Les Halles does not exist anymore. This once celebrated food market has been demolished, and on that site a gigantic, partially underground, shopping center was built in 1979. Two hundred stores, sixteen restaurants and many movie theaters and the unusual architecture make this now a tourist attraction.

I went to the shop a couple of hours before classes started in order to clean and tidy it up and occasionally, after classes, returned to it again for another two hours to do some more of the same. I was happy in my classes; people were most helpful; the war had left everyone with the desire to assist each other, in short, the mood was mellow and even when some food items were still scarce and some merchandise not readily available, Paris began again to be the City of Light.

My room, although very Spartan, was comfortable and I had some kind of burner on which I could heat water. I was introduced to the Nescafe my parents had sent, and a hot drink in my room whenever I wanted was a luxury I enjoyed. There was only a sink in the room but no shower on the premises. In order to take a bath, I had to go to a public bath house. There, for a nominal fee, I purchased a ticket, and would then be assigned to a small room with a bathtub which the attendant would fill and then leave. Sometimes I would have to wait until a room was vacant, and there was a limit on how long the room could be occupied. The only drawback was that during the winter, now thoroughly warmed up, I had to walk back to my room, a task I did not look forward to when it rained or snowed.

Occasionally I would drop into the U.S. Embassy to check on when my visa would be issued. During the middle of the winter, I came down with what I thought was a cold, but then I concluded that since I had severe coughing spells that I had bronchitis. I mentioned this in one of my letters to my parents, and I received by return mail some cough remedies which certainly eased the symptoms. I took it easy and for a few weeks rested as much as I could. This turned

out to have been the right decision, as at last the cough sub-
sided and I started to feel better and less tired.

Then, one day, I received my visa. Even when I actually
held it my hands, I had a hard time believing that this was
not a dream but reality. My parents had tried so very hard
to hasten this process, following up on every lead. They
even went to see Herbert Lehman, former Governor of New
York, who had gone to work for the U.S. State Department,
to plead my cause. A new problem arose: it was difficult to
obtain passage to the States. I was booked for passage on a
ship and it looked like it would be a long wait for me. The
date of my departure was constantly changed. To ensure
my passage, my parents also booked me on a plane.

Every day, I waited at the booking offices only to be told
in the vaguest of words that they just were not sure when
transportation would be available. Their parting words always were that they would call me if something would ma-
terialize. Finally, there was a seat available on a plane and
I notified my family of the specific date and then anxiously
counted the days until my departure.

Even this aspect of my journey to the "New World" developed a hitch; a day before I was to leave Paris, the airline notified me that my flight was canceled. I immediately
sent a telegram to my parents informing them of the delay
but was unable to give them a new date. They would call
me, the booking office promised, as soon as there was a seat
available, and I braced myself for a long wait. I was terribly
disappointed, had thought myself to be already over all the
hurdles and near my goal.

Now, I was afraid to leave my room for any length of time and sat around most of the next day. On the evening when I gave up on receiving notice, I decided, that for lack of anything else to do, I would wash my hair in the sink. No sooner did I rinse my hair when the call came, notifying me that there was a seat available, provided that I would be at the airport as soon as possible. I called a taxi immediately and was already downstairs waiting before it came. Once inside the taxi I implored the driver to get me to Orley quickly. Somehow, I had the presence of mind to dispatch a telegram to my family telling them that I would arrive on the following day and also gave them the flight number.

When I boarded the plane, my hair was still wet. After the plane took off, I glanced through the window and, when I saw what I thought to be flames coming from the plane, I panicked. I thought that it was ironic that after my having survived these last few years, I would now die in the plane which would have taken me to a new life. Apparently, my agitation was noticed, and I was calmed down by the crew, who also told me that this airplane, a Constellation, was perfectly safe and what I saw were the exhausts. There were very few passengers on the plane, probably not more than about twenty. Among them was the former French Premier, Leon Blum.

We stopped for refueling in Gander, Newfoundland, and then landed at La Guardia on March 15, 1946, after a flight of 22 hours. I was directed to a section which dealt with immigration and was asked where my luggage was. I pointed to the small shopping bag which contained all my possessions. I had packed a change of clothes, a memento, a part of my concentration camp outfit, a slip which was made out of blue and gray striped prison material; a silk scarf for my mother, and some perfume I had quickly purchased when I found out that I had a few Francs left. I could see that the custom inspector was surprised and did not even bother to search me but waved me through immediately and then I was reunited with my brother.

Harry was asked to pay the eight dollars that was required for entering this country. He found himself without cash and they finally accepted his check. Later he told me that he did not know for certain that I would be on this flight and he explained the circumstances to me. The previous day they had received my cable telling them that I would arrive on that day, but then, in the morning, another came saying that the flight was cancelled. He called the airline, only to find out that there was no flight list with the names of passengers available. He took a chance and drove to the airport anyway.

The mystery of the confusing messages was solved: my first telegram telling them of the cancellation had been sent as a night telegram and slow to arrive; the second advising them I was to arrive the following morning, was a more direct one and arrived faster, before the first. No wonder that everyone was confused.

Finally, in total euphoria, I was on my way to Mount Vernon to see my parents. No sooner did we open the front door before climbing a short flight of stairs, the most deli-

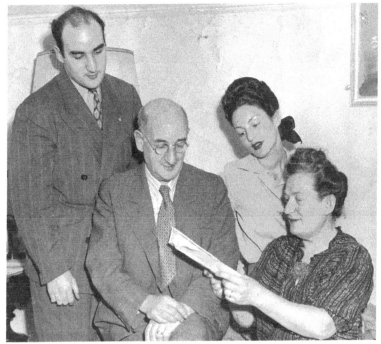

Family reunited. Charlotte and Harry look on as their parents, Anna and Stephan view their recently granted U.S. citizenship certificate. From a local newspaper article describing Charlotte's ordeal. It also notes Harry's recent return from military service in Italy.

cious odor wafted toward me, one that I had not smelled for many years, but dreamed of, talked of, and never forgotten, that of my mother's traditional Sabbath dinner, for it was Friday night! True to my mother's conviction that food is good for everything that ails you, and not only chicken soup, she must have attempted to cook enough to make up for all the years I had to go without. If anyone would have seen this scene of my homecoming in a movie, they would have described it as typically Hollywood staging.

The euphoria of our family being reunited was short lived. A few months later, the consequences of hardship and deprivation of the previous years surfaced. I had been suffering from fever and extreme fatigue for several weeks, attributing it to a cold. After a coughing spell which resulted in bleeding, I was admitted to the hospital and diagnosed as having Tuberculosis. I still considered myself lucky. Had X-rays been required before entering this country, I probably would have been diagnosed as already having the disease and I would not have been allowed to enter. I suspected, that during the winter months in Paris, what I assumed to have been a cold was the start of my illness.

The disease advanced at an alarming rate; I think the term "galloping" T.B. was used and a procedure, pneumothorax, was instituted. Air was injected to collapse the diseased lung temporarily until it healed. As some of the air was absorbed, monitored by fluoroscopy, more would be injected. The remaining treatment consisted of strict bed rest; I did not even sit up to eat, always keeping in mind that I wanted to breathe as shallowly as possible. The other lung, began to show a lesion, too. Later on I was transferred to a county hospital in which one entire wing was occupied by T.B. patients.

By the fall of 1947 complications set in and this form of treatment had to be abandoned. I had to submit to two operations, six weeks apart, in which several ribs were removed and most of the left lung was permanently collapsed. In the beginning of October, I was operated on for the first time. I remember that a few days after the second operation, the first experimental drug treatment for T.B. was initiated and tried on my roommate. This became the standard treat-

TB Ward, 1947

ment. I progressed, and under strict monitoring resumed more and more activities so that by summer of 1948, I was released as being fit enough to go back into the world. The "Seven Lean Years" were over!

A few words are necessary in regards to my marriage in Riga, which had never gotten off to a good start. We really did not have a chance to get to know each other well before we married in haste, and hardly were able to make the necessary adjustments to living with each other before the Nazis stormed Latvia a little more than a year later.

We still were together in the ghetto for four weeks until November 29, 1941, and then were separated when young, able-bodied men were sent to what later on was called the "little ghetto" and I was taken to prison. We found ourselves often on the same labor detail but always lived separately. We both were evacuated from Riga on August 6, 1944, and arrived at Stutthof at the same time. From there, Gena was taken to Buchenwald and survived the war. After I came to America, I was convinced that the prospect of a good marriage was slim and filed for divorce, which at first, he contested.

Epilogue

More than forty years have passed since the liberation and all this time I was reluctant to talk about the ghetto and camps. To my family, I just wanted to be acknowledged as the wife and mother, not as the survivor. To my friends and co-workers, I wanted to be just Charlotte, without anybody's perception to be influenced by my experiences. Still, there hardly have been situations at home or at work in which memories of those years would not surface. When our son Peter, at 18 months, had to be hospitalized I consoled myself that he was surrounded by love and care in contrast to the children in camp. When I taught nursery school and saw how, for some children, parting from their mothers brought tears, my thoughts turned to all the children who perished alone. Many things have been too painful or embarrassing to tell and the only time I opened up without reservation is when I was together with other survivors, in particular the few who were in Riga and Stutthof.

Occasionally, I am asked how I managed to survive. I cannot take any credit for that. In some instances, I found myself in favorable circumstances purely by chance, in others it seemed that I was "directed" to make certain, life-saving, split-second decisions. Today it takes me longer to select one of two heads of lettuce when shopping for groceries than it took me to make those decisions which may have influenced the outcome of my being alive in the next hour.

Looking at the statistics, realizing the small number of survivors, I was one of only 300 women who were spared during the 10 bloody days from November 28 to December 9, 1941. I would say that it was a miracle that I not only survived that week at all, but also the more than three years which followed when one day was almost a lifetime. The total count in the ghetto before that week was 33,000 men, women and children of which 27,000 perished during those bloody days. I was never able to find out how many of the 300 women were still alive at the end of the war; I am certain of only six others besides myself.

I have often wondered how those war years have affected me. As I never talked about them, I was never aware how I really felt. During the first few years of my second marriage I was afraid that I would run out of food and I stockpiled enough food on the shelves in the cellar to have lasted us for months during an emergency. The war was not over for me yet.

When I went to Europe in 1962, I had to stop off at the Frankfurt airport to change planes. As I got off the plane and walked to a different gate to make my connection, I was assailed by voices speaking German. I must have gone instantly into shock because I began to tremble violently and began to cry. My reaction astonished me, because of the fact that I always spoke German with my mother. So much for having everything under control.

Still, I feel guilty that I had survived, and I am not alone feeling that way. The question of why I did survive has never been answered. So, I searched to find a reason for being saved; and that, too, eluded me. And so, all I could aim for was to attempt in small ways and not always successfully to make life a little more pleasant for others. I am vigilant and speak out if I confront bigotry and injustice. For me, the worst hour of the year is on Yom Kippur, during Yizkor, the Memorial for the Dead.

A few times it has been said to me that I really must hate the German people. My reply was that if I did, then I must also indict the whole world who stood by idly and in apathy while ships were diverted, visas were not issued and churches kept silent. The United States had enough knowledge of the "Final Solution" but never once

Charlotte Arpadi Baum, July, 1985

increased the quota of visas or, later, attempted to bomb railroad tracks leading to extermination camps.

Yes, I am happy to be here in the United States. I still marvel at the fact that I can make derogatory comments about government issues, including heads of states, and not get arrested.

Now, aware that time for me is running out, I would like to document "My Story" so that future generations will know what had happened, and what can happen. And I have absolutely no doubt that it could happen again!

One can see that Jews in many countries, in particular the Islamic states, still face oppression and certain anti-Semitic organizations here, in the United States. and in other countries, are trying to establish themselves, preaching their philosophy of hate. This record is also an answer to those who attempt to refute that the Holocaust ever happened.

Nobel Laureate Elie Wiesel once said: "Whoever survives a test, whatever it may be, must tell the story. That is his duty." So here is mine.